How to Grow
House
Plants

By the Editors of Sunset Books and Sunset Magazine

Lane Publishing Co. • Menlo Park, California

Acknowledgments

For their helpful advice and assistance, we extend
special thanks to Patt and Jack Hudler, Dorothy Knecht,
Karyn McInnis, Lurlie Moore, and Daphne Smith.

Edited by Kathryn Arthurs

Artwork: Dinah James

Design: Roger Flanagan, Terrence Meagher

Cover: Complementary combination of house plants
adds interest to bookcase. Plants pictured
are (clockwise from top) Cissus antarctica, Coleus
blumei, Brassia maculata. Photographed by Ells Marugg.

Executive Editor, Sunset Books: David E. Clark

First Printing September 1976

Contents

Special features

Year-round gardening indoors

Two-story entry is perfect show place for house plant collection. Watering, misting chores can't damage floor.

Using plants indoors requires more than a good eye for decorating. Indoor gardeners want healthy, thriving house plants to accent various spots around their homes. To be a successful indoor gardener, you'll need to understand the conditions growing plants need to remain healthy: adequate light, correct temperatures, proper humidity level, and the right plant care. Providing these conditions is essential in bringing your house plants to their full potential.

What you need to know about both the esthetics and the care of house plants this chapter will tell you. Ideas for various ways of displaying plants—suspending them from walls or ceilings; setting large plants on the floor; placing them on shelves, tables, or plant stands—are also yours for the reading.

What makes plants grow?

Plant survival depends on two interacting processes, photosynthesis and respiration. The products created during one process are utilized in the cycle of the other. A third process, transpiration, causes plants to lose moisture. Understanding these plant processes and what conditions permit them to take place will help you find good indoor locations for growing house plants.

Photosynthesis and respiration

Photosynthesis is the process by which plants manufacture their own food. They take in energy from the sun or light source, carbon dioxide from the air, and water from the soil; these are combined to create plant sugars. Plant sugars are a versatile food; they can supply energy to the plant immediately, be stored as food for later use, or be used in building material within the plant body. Nutrients taken in from the soil or potting mix help in the production of plant sugars as well as in the growth of the plant.

While photosynthesis is at work, another process called respiration takes place simultaneously. The plant sugars (created by photosynthesis) are "burned" to create energy for all plant functions. Every portion of a plant—from the topmost leaves to the deepest roots—requires its share of energy to sustain itself. During respiration, oxygen is taken from the air; carbon dioxide is given off as a by-product.

These two processes set up a continuing cycle in which the products of one process are used in the function of the other. This is illustrated at right.

Transpiration

Transpiration is the giving off of a plant's collected moisture through the leaves. Unless this lost moisture is restored, the plant will soon wither and die. Because indoor plants are totally dependent upon their keeper for this needed moisture, good watering practices must be followed to offset transpiration. Watering house plants is discussed in detail on pages 15-16.

One benefit of transpiration is the humidity created when moisture evaporates from leaf surfaces. Grouping house plants together can create a "mini-atmosphere" of humidity (see page 17 for further information).

Treat them right

A good location for growing plants indoors provides the light, temperature, and atmospheric conditions plants need to survive. A house plant placed in a good spot and given the proper care has every opportunity to thrive.

Plants are individual

Each house plant has unique needs as to light, temperature, and humidity. The best way to choose a plant for your house is to first decide on its future location. Study possible indoor locations by asking yourself these questions: Would a house plant enhance this particular spot? How much light is available? What is the average temperature? Are there seasonal changes in light or temperature? How much humidity is present?

Once you answer these questions you will have a profile of your location. The next step is selecting a plant to fill it. Study the Plant Selection Guide, pages 26-79, to find the plant or plants that prefer the environment you have to offer.

If you wish to grow plants unsuited to your location, you can modify the spot to fit a plant's needs. You may provide artificial light, extra humidity (for ways to increase humidity, see pages 16-17), or adjust the room's temperature. Still another solution is to move the plant daily to a location more suited to plant growth and then later return it to the location it decorates. This practice, however, can be time consuming and not too practical.

Some of us are impulse buyers, choosing a plant for its colorful foliage or interesting flower and giving no thought to its growing needs. If this describes many of your plant purchases, try to find out as much about the plant as possible (either from the Plant Selection Guide, pages 26-79, or from nursery personnel or the salesperson where you purchased it). Then find or adapt a location for it. Remember that impulse purchases will probably create more work for you and will not always prove successful.

If you begin your house plant shopping with the location firmly in mind and select a plant with the individual needs to fit it, you're on the right track for successful house plant tending.

Light is the limiting factor

Plants need light for photosynthesis (see these pages) but in varying degrees. Blooming plants usually require more light than foliage plants. So do plants that set fruit.

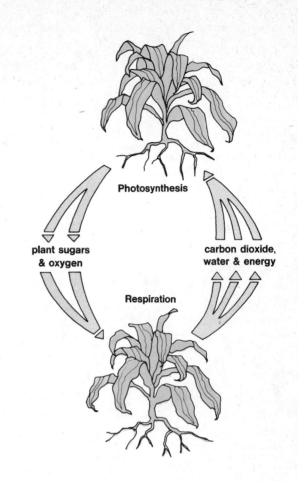

Photosynthesis *cycle shown by top plant; respiration, by bottom plant. Arrows indicate interaction between two.*

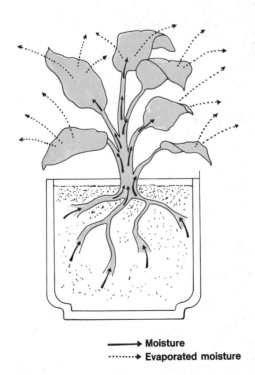

⎯⎯→ Moisture
┈┈┈→ Evaporated moisture

Arrows *show transpiration cycle; water comes into plant roots, goes through plant, evaporates off leaf surfaces.*

Some plants require direct sunlight; others prefer filtered or low light situations. Another light factor is the amount of time a plant receives light daily. For some plants, shortening days indicate winter and signal the start of their dormancy or rest period. For others, such as chrysanthemums and Christmas cactus, day length controls their blooming cycle. You can control day length, if you wish, by adding artificial light or by placing plants in a dark room. To affect the plant's cycle, the addition or deprivation of light must be consistent.

It is best to place plants in a location that provides the light situation they prefer (for light requirements of individual house plants, see the Plant Selection Guide, pages 26-79). But if you decide to place house plants in a location offering less than optimum light, your plant care must change. Since a plant's energy and growth depend upon light, don't expect maximum performance from these plants. Plants growing in limited light should receive less water and fertilizer than identical plants growing in better locations. Repotting should be put off as long as possible. By withholding water and fertilizer and postponing repotting, you will maintain these plants, rather than encouraging them to grow. Maintained plants given limited light, water, and fertilizer should last as long as other house plants; they will remain about the same size and shape indefinitely. The best candidates for maintenance growing situations are those that can tolerate filtered or low light.

Types of available light. The type of light found in indoor situations falls into four main categories:

Sun means direct sunlight coming through a window. An east facing exposure allows morning sun and generally coolish afternoon temperatures. A west window permits afternoon sun with warmer temperatures. A south facing exposure offers sun and warm temperatures most of the day (this is the brightest exposure). Direct sunlight magnified by window glass may raise the temperature to stifling heights that could burn foliage. Most house plants that prefer to bask in sunlight like to be set back from the windowpane.

Bright light can be found in the interior portions of a sunny room or from light reflected from light-colored walls. A plant that prefers this exposure needs it constantly throughout the daylight hours. A north facing exposure provides bright light with no sun.

Filtered or diffused light is light coming through a lightweight curtain over a window or light that filters into a window through trees or plants growing outdoors. Overhangs or patio roofs also block or filter light.

Low light usually refers to dark parts in room interiors, dark corners, or areas without windows. There are few plants that can tolerate these situations; most will need additional light. These areas are prime candidates for artificial lighting.

Using artificial lighting. If the location you choose for growing plants needs supplemental lighting to be effective, providing artificial lighting may be the answer. Plants can also benefit from a combination of natural and artificial light during the short, gray days of winter.

Plain fluorescent lights can supply sufficient light for plant growth. They can also be used in combination with the less expensive incandescent bulbs. Incandescent lights should not be used alone; they are not strong enough in the red and blue color bands that plants need, and they generate too much heat for sensitive plants.

Some indoor gardeners grow house plants totally under artificial lights. As long as the artificial lighting provides the same intensity and quality of light found in natural sunlight, and your plants are exposed to it for a sufficient period each day, they should thrive. Special fluorescent tubes, developed to simulate actual sunlight rays, can stimulate plants to bloom, produce fruit, and set seeds. These are slightly more expensive than regular fluorescent tubes and are readily available.

Whether you buy a lighting unit or make one, provide some method of adjusting the height to allow for plant growth and different-size containers. Start with the tubes 6 to 12 inches above the foliage. If the foliage bunches together unnaturally, plants are receiving too much light. If they become leggy, they need more light. Fluorescent lighting will not harm plants, so the light may be set as close as needed.

Fixtures need a white or foil reflector to direct light onto plants. When placing plants under it, remember the light is strongest at the center of the tube. Several fluorescent tubes placed side by side are best; one tube alone will not support plant life that depends solely on this light. A standard amount of light for all plants is 15 to 20 watts of light for every square foot of growing surface.

Most plants require a period of darkness every 24 hours (even plants need their sleep). Most foliage plants need 10 to 12 hours of light a day; flowering plants require 16. A regular schedule is important to healthy plant growth. An inexpensive timer can be used to regulate the lights.

Some like it hot

And some plants like cool temperatures. Luckily, the majority of house plants adjust readily to normal indoor temperatures. Since people as well as plants occupy rooms, it's best to select plants that prefer the same temperature levels you do. Unless you wish to provide a special plant room or a greenhouse that caters to specific temperature needs, leave finicky plants to more advanced gardeners.

Temperature levels found in most home situations fall into three main categories: cool (55°-65°), average (65°-75°), and warm (75°-85°).

Avoid exposing plants to drastic temperature changes and drafts. Windows may be many degrees hotter or colder than the room interior. Check the temperature near windows where plants are kept during extreme weather conditions (either hot or cold conditions, since both extremes can be devastating), and move plants if necessary. Other locations to avoid are on or near heat registers, radiators, or fireplaces, or in the direct blast of air conditioning.

Humidity levels are closely related to house temperatures: the warmer the air, the faster humidity in the air is dispelled. (Warm temperatures also speed up transpiration in plants; see page 5.) This is especially true when a home's central heating unit is in use, creating a hot, dry atmosphere. Many plants we grow indoors need humidity to survive, and they depend on us to provide it. Ways to increase humidity levels indoors are discussed on pages 16-17.

Indoor landscaping

Whether you use plants strictly as decorative accents (and replace them when they begin to look forlorn) or find caring for plants as enjoyable as having them grace your home, your approach to growing and displaying plants indoors will be as unique and individual as your own personality. Your use of house plants is limited only by available space and your imagination.

As with everything else, conventional plant placements are rapidly being replaced by innovative displays. Plant containers (discussed on pages 8-11) and the necessity of watering (see pages 15-16 for further information) will also need to be considered.

The following section describes some of the ways house plants can be displayed. Use the suggestions or adapt them to your particular situation.

The house tree. Large, treelike plants make a strong statement in your house. Planted in capacious containers, they can accent an entry or a view, fill an empty corner, hide a problem area, or divide indoor spaces into smaller, more usable areas.

Care can present a problem. Sheer size necessitates keeping large plants stationary; watering, fertilizing, and maintenance will take place on the spot. Another problem is to protect your floor or carpet from water damage — a "buffer zone" (see page 10) is a good solution.

Hanging plants. Any house plant with a drooping or spreading growth habit can be hung to advantage. Possible locations are in windows, corners of rooms, and around skylights. Just hang them out of the way of foot traffic—bumping into a heavy hanging plant isn't healthy for the person or the plant.

How to suspend the plant and how to water it once it's up are two major challenges. A well-watered house plant and it's container can weigh up to 50 pounds. It's best to place the hook or bracket that holds the plant in a wall stud or ceiling joist for maximum support. If the best location is nowhere near a stud or joist and you must rely on gypsum wallboard to hold the plant, use a toggle bolt or a spreading fastener; these help provide better weight distribution.

Whenever possible, use plastic plant containers for your hanging plants—they weigh much less than clay or ceramic pots, they won't absorb any moisture, and plants in them require less water.

Watering is still another dilemma. A watered plant will drip. To prevent this, either provide a drip saucer (see page 10) to catch excess water (a commercial tray that clips onto the bottom of hanging pots is available) or take the plant down to water it and let it drain completely before rehanging.

Put your plants on a pedestal. Plants set on a plant stand become a living piece of sculpture. Whether the pedestal is metal and glass, intricately turned wrought iron, a small wooden table, a turned wooden post, or a marble column, both the stand and the plant will receive compliments. Plants on plant stands are best placed in an empty corner, in a window, or on a fairly blank wall so nothing distracts from their beauty.

Care presents few problems. Drip saucers and the plant stand surface protect furniture, floors, and carpets from water damage. Be sure your stand is stable; a top-heavy plant could cause a precariously balanced stand to topple.

Placing plants around the room. Whether you use plants on tables, bookshelves, mantels, or other interior surfaces, the plants and their containers form a decorative accent. Choose healthy plants that are sized proportionally for the space they will occupy. Attractive foliage or colorful flowers are always a bonus.

Buyer's Guide to Healthy Plants

When you have an urge to buy a house plant, you need to consider two things: the plant itself and the shop or nursery where it's sold. Be choosy; don't settle for the first plant you see.

Finding a reputable house plant dealer is the first step. You may have good luck with bargain plants, but it's best to buy from a nursery, plant boutique, or florist shop where plants are given proper treatment.

If you are a wise shopper, you'll size up house plant and dealer along these lines:

1. Survey the general plant selection. Do most plants seem healthy and happy? Overall excellence of products usually signifies good merchandise and proper care of house plants.

2. Look at the plant itself. Does it look healthy? Is it free from leaf damage and pests? Is the color good? Does it have a pleasing shape? Is the leaf size consistent? Does it show any new growth? If the answer to all these questions is "Yes," your choice is probably a good one.

3. Check to see if the plant is potbound. If any plant roots are peeking through the drainage hole, the plant has been in that pot too long. It's best to choose a different one.

4. Choose a plant the size you want it. If you want a large house plant, don't buy a small version and wait for it to grow. It could take months or years. A larger plant that is better established should adapt to a new environment more readily.

Container ins and outs

Pebbles *add pleasing finishing touch to decorative sleeve planting by hiding dirt, clay pot rim, rock filler.*

You've found the perfect house plant and selected its new location. The next step? Select a container and a potting mix—then put them all together.

A plant container does more than hold the potting mix and house plant: it also provides decoration. Plants used indoors become room accessories, and their containers help considerably in making them effective. Choose containers that will suit the plants and enhance their location.

This chapter provides you with information on available plant containers, potting mixes, and step-by-step planting techniques, as well as planting in drainless and self-watering containers and using decorative sleeves.

The choices are many

When selecting a plant container, the indoor gardener need no longer settle for the commonplace red clay pot. A myriad of choices is possible.

With the rebirth of house plant popularity, manufacturers have responded by offering a wide variety of containers in many sizes, shapes, colors, and materials. Indoor gardeners can also utilize decorative sleeves—large containers of metal, wicker, or ceramic too special for direct planting—to hold potted plants for display purposes.

Your main consideration in choosing a container is your plant's growing needs. The size of the container will be determined by the plant's size. Put your plant in a pot that's the same size as its present container or in one that is ½ to 1 inch larger in diameter. Avoid potting a plant in too small or too large a container.

Different types of containers offer growing advantages for plants with special needs. Plastic pots and other nonporous containers keep soil damp the longest —a good situation for moisture-loving plants. Porous pots, such as red clay, allow air circulation around root systems; this hastens moisture loss in potting mix, good for plants that prefer to dry out between waterings. Study your house plant's growth requirements very carefully and then consult the Plant Selection Guide on pages 26-79 before purchasing its container.

Look for house plant containers in nurseries, indoor plant stores, garden supply stores, antique stores, craft shops or craft fairs, hardware stores, stores that specialize in home accessories, or any other store that might sell garden or house plant supplies.

Types of containers

Before purchasing your house plant's container, familiarize yourself with the possibilities. You'll find almost as many different kinds of containers available as house plants.

Some general points to keep in mind: 1) Try to find containers with drainage holes. You can plant in a drainless container, but plant care is much more difficult (see page 13 for instructions). 2) Choose the container that best meets your plant's growth needs. 3) Select a container that will accent your interior decoration. Plants and their containers become an important part of the rooms they occupy and should be used to create the best possible effect. 4) Try to purchase a drip saucer (see page 10) at the same time you buy the container. Size and compatibility are easier to judge with the container in hand.

Clay pots. That old standby, the red clay pot, continues to be popular. It's inexpensive, easy to find, and available in many shapes and sizes. The earthy color (besides red, clay pots are sometimes available in shades of brown or gray) and texture blend well with most furniture styles and don't overshadow the plant.

Because they are porous, clay pots absorb moisture and permit air circulation. They are great for beginning gardeners since it is difficult (but not impossible) to overwater plants in them.

If plants are overfertilized, excess salts appear as a white crust on the pot sides. In areas where the water has a heavy salt concentration, the excess salts leach out, also forming a white crust on pot sides. A nonporous container cannot give you these problem signals.

Plastic pots. Modern man's answer to pottery is plastic. Plastic containers are easy to clean, lightweight even when watered, inexpensive to buy, and available in a wide variety of colors, shapes, and sizes. One novel container is made of clear plastic, exposing the potting mix and root system.

Nonporous plastic pots may create watering problems. They do not absorb any moisture or permit air circulation. Since watered plants in plastic pots remain moist longer than plants in porous containers and need watering less frequently, plastic pots are the best choice for moisture-loving plants. Until watering plants has become second nature, though, the beginning indoor gardener may find porous pots easier to use.

If wide slits on the container bottom serve as drainage holes, use a thin layer of stones or pebbles instead of pot shards for crocking.

Glazed ceramic pots. Available in many colors and sometimes vividly decorated with patterns or pictures, glazed ceramic pots are quite ornamental. Prices vary according to size and decoration.

Glazed containers, like plastic pots, are nonporous and may present watering problems to the beginner. If you find the perfect glazed pot but are hesitant to buy it because of possible watering difficulties, use it as a decorative sleeve (see page 10 for directions).

Metal containers. With the renewed interest in indoor gardening, an increasing number of people use house plants as decorative objects. Plants in metal containers of copper, brass, silver or silverplate, pewter, polished steel, iron, or aluminum are elegant enough to suit any decor.

For various reasons, most metal containers are best used as decorative sleeves (see page 10). Since many metals tarnish, they may require periodic cleaning or polishing. If excess water is left standing indefinitely in the pot, it could corrode the metals. If your container is valuable, line it with heavy plastic or place a drainage saucer inside to avoid water damage.

Metal containers rarely have drainage holes. If you decide to plant directly into your metal pot, drainage material (see page 13) must be provided to capture any excess moisture created by regular waterings. If you are lucky enough to find a metal pot with proper drainage holes, treat it as a normal container when planting. Be sure to provide a saucer or tray to catch any water runoff.

Plant roots that touch the sides or bottom of a copper pot will die. This shouldn't radically affect the plant's health, since the remaining roots will live.

Wooden containers. Though more generally used outdoors, wooden containers are relatively inexpensive and available in many sizes, shapes, and wood types.

Stained or varnished wood is usually nonporous. Untreated wood containers can be porous and, like clay pots, should be soaked before you plant in them. If drainage holes are present, place a waterproof saucer under the pot to catch excess water.

If your wooden container is slatted, the sides may not be watertight. This could create a seepage problem that would be unattractive, as well as hard on furniture surfaces. It's best to use these containers as decorative sleeves (see page 10) rather than planting in them directly.

Baskets. Plants and basketry seem to be made for each other. Baskets can be found in a profusion of shapes, sizes, and price ranges. Though usually constructed of natural materials in shades of beige or brown, some woven containers are painted or stained in a variety of colors.

Since baskets aren't watertight, they should be used as decorative sleeves (see page 10). Unless a saucer to catch water runoff can be placed inside the basket, watered plants will leak, probably ruining furniture surfaces and eventually the basket.

A few baskets can be purchased with metal inserts, permitting planting in them directly. Since these inserts do not have drainage holes, treat them as drainless containers when planting.

Self-watering containers. If you find watering house plants a nuisance or if you travel frequently and must leave your plants alone, self-watering containers may be the answer. These innovative containers are usually constructed of plastic. They have a reservoir for storing water and a method of tapping this stored water when the potting soil dries out. Moving through capillary action, water is drawn up into the pot by either a sensing device or a fiber wick until the potting mix becomes evenly moist. When the potting mix dries out again, the cycle is repeated.

Use the self-watering container as a decorative sleeve (see page 10) or plant directly into it.

Eclectic containers. If your taste leans to the unusual or the unexpected, you can put plants in containers originally designed for other purposes. Cookie jars, ice buckets, pitchers, coffee pots, jars, watering cans, or anything else with enough space to hold potting mix and a plant can be transformed into unique containers. You need only imagination and courage.

Since these containers were not designed to hold plants, they will not have drainage holes. Follow the planting instructions for drainless containers on page 13 or use them as decorative sleeves (see below).

Catch that drip!

If you correctly water a house plant growing in a container that has proper drainage, you're going to have a drip problem. Any excess water that the potting mix can't retain during the normal watering will run out the drainage holes. Wherever you display house plants, this runoff will probably be troublesome. The most efficient solution is to provide a saucer to catch the excess water.

Many containers are sold with matching saucers. Whenever possible, buy a drip saucer or tray at the same time you purchase a container. With other plant containers, it's up to the indoor gardener to find a suitable drip saucer. Look for unobtrusive saucers or trays. Though a mismatched saucer may protect furniture surfaces, it can ruin the visual effect of the house plant. Pads or mats may also be used to protect interior surfaces.

Part of the runoff problem can be solved at watering time. Take house plants to a sink for watering; then let them drain in the sink for a while (at least 10 minutes). The majority of excess water should drain into the sink, not into the drip saucer. This method of watering does not eliminate the need for a drip saucer, though.

If your drip saucer or tray is made of a porous material, such as red clay, it can absorb moisture. You can paint the interior of a clay saucer with silicone paint to waterproof it; this eliminates the absorption problem. Water sitting in nonporous saucers, such as plastic or glazed ceramic, may cause condensation on the saucer's exterior. If the saucers with absorbed moisture or condensation remain in one spot long enough, the contact may eventually ruin furniture surfaces or rot carpets.

Many indoor gardeners protect surfaces by creating a "buffer zone" between drip saucers and furniture, floors, or carpets. This buffer zone forms an air space in which any absorbed moisture or moisture caused by condensation can be dissipated. Coasters, mats, blocks of wood, metal or wooden plant holders, or any other means of raising the plant container and saucer off furniture or carpet surfaces create a buffer zone. This created air space helps eliminate the chance of any water damage.

Using decorative sleeves

A decorative sleeve is any container that an already-potted house plant is set into for display purposes. The decorative sleeve has many advantages: 1) Valuable or easily damaged containers are protected from any damage that might be caused by direct planting. 2) A sick plant can be replaced quickly by a healthy plant, avoiding the need to transplant, which is time-consuming for you and hard on an ailing plant. 3) Many decorative sleeves are watertight, eliminating the need for a drip saucer or tray. 4) If you display plants in a poor growing location, such as a dark hall, you can rotate several plants between a good growing location and the location of a decorative sleeve placed in a spot with bad lighting. This keeps your plants in a healthy condition.

Utilizing decorative sleeves is easy. The sleeve should always be at least an inch larger in diameter

Decorative sleeves: *Ceramic, copper, or wicker can show off your plants*

Decorative sleeves *display potted plants. From left: layer of pebbles supports potted plant inside ceramic sleeve; copper bucket contains plant raised by brick; clay pots lift plant to top of wicker basket.*

How to Make Baskets Hold Water

Though woven baskets make good house plant containers, watering the plants presents the problem of leakage. Lining the basket with a plastic bag or aluminum foil is a possible solution, but inevitably the plastic tears or the foil breaks. The best answer is to coat the basket interior with polyester resin and strips of newspaper.

You'll need clear polyester resin and hardener (they come in separate containers), a brush, acetone to clean the brush, and some newspaper strips. A quart of resin is enough for about three baskets of wastepaper basket size.

Cut the newspaper into 4-inch wide strips the length of the basket bottom diameter plus about 10 inches (the strips should go up about 5 inches on each side). Make sure you work outdoors or in a very well-ventilated area; the resin fumes are both strong-smelling and dangerous. Protect your hands with gloves.

To prepare one basket, thoroughly mix about a third of the resin with a proportionate amount of hardener according to the directions on the can (if you're doing a very large basket, mix more of the resin). Brush the mixture onto the basket bottom and up the sides about 5 inches. Place a strip of newspaper to cover this; then brush resin onto the paper.

Continue with the alternate pattern of resin and paper strips (crisscrossing the strips to cover the bottom) until you have about eight layers of paper. Pour any remaining resin mixture into the bottom of the basket and let it harden. Check to be sure you have a complete seal. If there's any leakage when you pour in water, let the basket dry and then mix up some more resin and recoat the paper-covered area.

Once the basket has been waterproofed, it's ready for a house plant. Either plant directly into the basket following directions for planting in a drainless container (see page 13 for information) or use the basket as a decorative sleeve container. Place plants planted in clay pots or other containers into the basket. A layer of rocks or a drip saucer will keep the pot from sitting in water.

---

than the plant's container to allow for good air circulation. Put the potted house plant into the sleeve. If it sits too low in the sleeve, prop it up. Bricks, other clay pots turned upside down, layers of small rocks or pebbles, sphagnum moss, or any material that will raise the potted plant to the proper level can be used. This also allows for drainage, keeping plants in decorative sleeves from sitting in water. Some examples of utilizing decorative sleeves are shown at left.

If the runoff from normal watering could damage your decorative sleeve, line it with heavy plastic or provide a drip saucer inside the sleeve under the potted plant as a preventive measure.

Some indoor gardeners also line the space between the plant container and the sleeve to give the illusion of direct planting. Sphagnum moss or pebbles are commonly used; loosely packed, they still permit adequate air circulation around the container. A top mulch of pebbles or bark covering both the soil surface of the plant and the liner helps add to this illusion (see photograph on page 8).

Filling the pot

Potting mix is the all-important ingredient for healthy plants. It forms the medium in which plants live and grow; it provides the initial nutrients plants need; and it permits moisture retention while allowing any excess water to drain away.

Commercial potting mixes

For most indoor gardeners, buying a package of prepared potting mix is the most efficient method of selecting house plant soil. Potting mix is sold in varying sized packages, so you can purchase only the amount you need at the time. (Reseal any leftover potting mix in the package for use later.)

Use a commercial mix specifically formulated for house plants. It temporarily provides the nutrients that plants need; you can replenish these nutrients when necessary with a house plant fertilizer (see pages 17-18). The packaged potting mix has been sterilized to eliminate any pests or diseases that might be present. These mixes are readily available at nurseries, indoor plant stores, or other stores where garden supplies are sold.

Some lightweight mixes need to be moistened before planting. Squeeze a handful of soil in your fist; the mix should be damp enough to form a compact ball when you release it, yet not be dripping wet. If the mix is dry and crumbly, add enough water to the mix to make it cohesive.

If you want to make your own

If purchasing a commercial potting mix in a plastic bag isn't your idea of returning to the soil indoors, you can make your own. Blend equal amounts of coarse sand (be sure to buy washed sand; the salt in unwashed sea sand may damage tender plants), garden loam or good garden topsoil, and peat moss, leaf mold, or fir bark.

Transplanting: *Step-by-step directions*

1. Remove plant *and root ball intact from original container.*

2. Cover drainage hole *with pebbles or pot shards; add some potting mix.*

3. Fill container *with soil until root ball surface is near pot rim.*

4. Center root ball *and steady it as you fill in sides with potting mix.*

5. Thump pot *carefully on working surface to settle potting mix.*

6. Smooth soil surface *gently with fingers, avoiding plant stem area.*

To each 2 quarts of this mix, add ½ cup each charcoal and perlite.

Every ingredient in your potting mix has a purpose. Garden loam or topsoil contains particles of clay that hold fertilizing materials in an available state for plant roots. Sand, perlite, and leaf mold hold air around the roots, which is essential to good plant growth. Leaf mold also provides some nutrients. Charcoal bits keep the soil "sweet." These ingredients are usually available at most nurseries, garden supply stores, or indoor plant stores.

Any potting mix that you make yourself which contains garden soil must be sterilized. Garden loam or topsoil may contain pests, weed seeds, or plant diseases; sterilizing the mix eliminates these problems.

Follow these steps to sterilize your soil: 1) Mix all ingredients thoroughly. 2) Dampen the mix slightly with water; then spread it—no more than 4 inches deep—in shallow ovenproof pans. 3) Place the filled pans in a 180° oven and bake for at least 2 hours.

An alternate method is to cover the soil-filled pans with kitchen foil or clear baking wrap and seal. Insert a cooking thermometer through the center of the covering into the soil but not touching the pan. Place in the oven and heat until the soil temperature reaches 180°; keep the temperature at that level—no higher—for 30 minutes.

Prepare yourself for the nasty odor of baking soil. Luckily this odor isn't lasting. Remove the sterilized soil from the oven and let it air for a few days. Store it in sturdy paper or plastic bags.

Step-by-step planting

Potting brings it all together: your house plant, its new container, and the potting mix in which it will live. Before you begin to repot, have all the necessary materials ready and waiting. Finding yourself out of potting mix with the container half filled is frustrating.

Container preparation

Always plant in a clean container. Wash containers in soap and water; rinse them well to remove any soap film.

Resurrected containers, especially red clay pots, may require scrubbing with a wire or a stiff-bristled brush to remove any clinging soil or salt and algae buildup.

Soak all porous containers (such as red clay pots) in water prior to planting. Dry, porous containers may rob moisture from the potting mix and the newly transplanted plant. Immerse the pots in water for an hour or so; then let them dry for a few minutes.

Never put a plant in too large a container; you'll have too much soil for too few roots. The roots can't extract water from the extra soil, and the surplus moisture may eventually rot the roots. Choose a container the same size as the one holding your house plant or one only slightly larger—a pot ½ to 1 inch larger in diameter is the maximum. If your present container is larger than 10 inches in diameter, you may wish to use a somewhat larger pot to avoid frequent transplanting.

Planting procedures

Transplanting is a messy business, so work in an easy-to-clean area. Work quickly to avoid transplanting shock to the plant. If you are interrupted, cover the exposed root ball with damp towels and return to the transplanting as soon as possible.

Gather together the house plant, the potting mix, the cleaned container, and any other needed materials and begin the transplanting:

1) Remove the plant from its present container, keeping the root ball intact. Knock it out according to the instructions on page 20.

Plants in metal nursery containers can be cut out. Slit the sides of the container, pull them away from the plant, and remove the root ball. Use tin snips or a can cutter or ask the nurseryman to do it for you.

2) Place pot shards (curved, broken bits of old clay pots) or pebbles over the drain hole (if you use pebbles, be sure they can't completely plug the drainage hole). This prevents the potting mix from draining out of the pot when the plant is watered. If you use pot shards, place them over the drainage hole so the curved surface faces as shown in the illustration on page 12.

3) Put enough potting mix in the pot to bring the surface of the root ball about ½ inch below the container rim. (You may want to leave more space in larger pots to keep things in proportion.) This level works best for watering plants. See illustration 3.

4) Center the root ball in the container and fill in the sides with potting mix. Occasionally, thump the container on your working surface to settle in the new soil (see illustrations 4 and 5). Continue to add potting mix until the sides are level with the root ball surface. Be careful not to bury the root ball—plants can suffocate, too.

5) Smooth out the surface of the new potting mix with your fingers. Don't push down on the root ball or the plant stem; this could damage fragile hair roots.

6) Water your newly potted plant thoroughly; then step back and admire. Once your plant adjusts to its new container, move it to its permanent location.

Soil layers *inside a drainless container are shown: (A) potting mix, (B) charcoal, (C) drainage material.*

Planting in a drainless container

Putting a house plant in a container without a drainage hole isn't ideal, but it can be done. Problems arise when the plant is watered; once in, the water has no escape. The solution is to provide a drainage layer inside the container to act as a holding tank for the excess moisture.

Place a layer of small rocks or pebbles in the bottom of the container. This layer should take up about one quarter of the total container volume. (You can also use small pieces of lava or "feather rock" or broken bits of clay pots for the drainage material.) The drainage layer allows water to seep through the soil and retains it until the moisture can be utilized by the plant or until it evaporates. Another advantage of the drainage layer is that it keeps the plant roots from sitting in soggy soil and permits the roots to obtain oxygen.

Spread a thin layer of charcoal bits directly over the drainage layer. Charcoal keeps the soil "sweet" by absorbing any noxious by-products created in decaying matter in the soil or potting mix.

Begin putting in the potting mix and proceed with the transplanting as described on page 12. The various layers used in a drainless container are shown above.

The adjustment period

A newly potted plant needs a respite from its normal environment. Adjusting to a new container can be traumatic for a plant.

Place the well-watered plant in a cool, sunless spot for several days. If it wilts, don't rewater unless the potting mix is completely bone dry at least an inch below the surface. Try misting to rejuvenate the plant. Or create a greenhouse atmosphere by sealing the plant, pot and all, in a plastic bag. (A sun-loving plant is an exception; place it immediately in its permanent location.)

Once it has adjusted to potting, move your plant to its permanent location.

Meeting your house plant's needs

Plant care *is an individual matter. Each plant has different watering, light, temperature, and fertilizing needs.*

Like any working unit—either living or mechanical—a plant needs proper maintenance to function normally. A plant grown indoors in a pot is completely dependent upon its caretaker for light, water, and nutrients. It requires the right amount of water, pruning to stay a reasonable size, repotting when its container becomes restrictive, and protection when diseases or pests attack.

This chapter gives you the instructions needed to maintain healthy house plants. It explains in detail the need for humidity, watering, fertilizing, pruning, and repotting, and it tells you how to inspect plants for possible problems. Consistent and careful attention to your plants' needs will allow them to function properly in their indoor environment.

Keep your eye on them

Inspecting house plants on a day-to-day basis or at regular intervals is a habit worth developing. Just a few minutes a day will help keep your plants in peak condition. This careful attention also enables you to correct most problems before they become major.

Ask yourself several questions during the routine check: 1) Does the plant need watering? 2) Has dust accumulated on the leaves? 3) Are any brown or dying leaves visible? 4) Is there any sign of a pest infestation? If the answer to any of these questions is "Yes," see the appropriate section below for a solution.

Watering frequency. Plants require varying amounts of water. Some like to be constantly moist; others prefer to dry out between waterings. Know your plant's water preference; the Plant Selection Guide on pages 26-79 includes the necessary watering information for most common house plants.

There are several methods of checking the amount of moisture present in the potting mix. Experiment until you find the best method for you. Methods of checking moisture levels in potted plants are discussed on page 16.

Dust accumulation. Plants—like furniture—benefit from regular dusting. Wash dirty leaves individually with plain water on a soft cloth or cotton. Always support a leaf with one hand and gently wipe off dust with the other.

Some plant keepers recommend occasional showers for their plants; use a spray attachment in a sink, a hose with a sprayer in the yard, or a bathroom shower. If you have a water softener, spray the plant outdoors with a hose, since water from outdoor faucets usually by-passes the water softener. Be sure to let plants drip dry before returning them to their normal places. Remember to limit outdoor excursions for tender house plants to the warmer seasons of the year.

Daily misting (see page 16) also helps keep dust from building up on plant foliage.

Brown or dying leaves. Keep your house plants looking fresh and healthy by removing any unsightly leaves with scissors or a sharp knife. Dead or dying leaves ruin the plant's appearance and may invite unwanted pests or disease. Removing dead leaves or branches also makes room for new growth.

Many leaves develop brown tips or edges, usually caused by a lack of humidity. Some indoor gardeners recommend trimming these unsightly edges off to keep up appearances. Use sharp scissors to cut off brown tips or edges; try to follow the natural leaf shape so the trim isn't obvious. Of course, this trimming won't correct the problem; it merely improves the plant's looks. Try to correct the situation as soon as possible. Causes of brown leaf tips and edges are discussed on page 23.

Pests. Most pests that attack house plants are small and hard to see. Your first indication of a problem will probably be poor plant health, which shows up as yellow or dying foliage, stunted growth, or curled or distorted foliage. Examine sickly plants closely. If pests seem to be the problem, refer to the section on pests and their control (see pages 23-25) for a solution. If you find no sign of small creatures on your sickly plant, make sure your plant is receiving the care and culture it requires. To familiarize yourself with your plant's requirements, see the Plant Selection Guide on pages 26-79.

How to water wisely

Watering is perhaps the most important service you can give your house plants. More plants fail from improper watering than from any other cause. The best way to avoid overwatering—the most common watering offense—is to know each plant's watering needs.

Watering is usually done in the morning. Many gardeners fill their watering cans the night before to allow the water to reach room temperature. This also permits any chlorine to evaporate.

If your water is softened in a water softener or if it's remarkably hard or tastes of salts or minerals, use bottled or distilled water. If your outdoor water faucets by-pass the water softener, draw the water there. Be sure to let the water reach room temperature before using it on plants. Some plant lovers catch rainwater in a cistern and water their plants with it.

"How much water?" is the first question most people ask when acquiring a plant. Most indoor plant specialists will respond evasively. Typical answers are, "As much as it needs"; "Not too much, yet not too little"; and the all-time favorite—"It depends." Watering is indeed a very individual matter. How much and how often you water a plant will depend on the nature of the plant and the environment it grows in. Water when

your plant needs it, not according to a schedule that's convenient for you.

Factors that affect watering

Since no two plants use water at exactly the same pace, many factors beyond the control of you or your plant will affect the amount of water it needs. Yet some of these factors—the type of container you select, for example—you *can* control and use to your plant's advantage.

The seasons. In winter, when days are short and skies often gray, house plants generally need less water than during the summertime. Some plants respond to winter by retreating into a state of listlessness. They don't require much water; instead, give them dry aid and comfort by continuing your routine inspections and making sure they have adequate light. When your listless plant perks up, resume its normal care.

Plant dormancy. Some plants have a season for going completely dormant. Dormancy is a period of inactivity or nongrowth. The foliage of most tuberous and bulbous plants (the plants most likely to have dormant periods) begins to yellow after the plants bloom. Gradually withhold water from these plants until the foliage is dry. Then store the pots with the tubers or bulbs in a cool, dry, out-of-the-way spot. When new growth appears, restore the plant to its customary place.

Containers. The container you choose to hold your plant will affect the amount of water needed and how often you apply it. (Plant containers are discussed in more detail on pages 9-10.)

Red clay pots are porous, absorbing moisture and permitting good air circulation. Plants growing in clay pots tend to use more water and need it more frequently than plants in other types of containers. Moisture level of plants in clay pots will need to be checked frequently.

Plastic pots are nonporous; potting mix in them tends to retain moisture for longer periods than mix in clay pots. Overwatering can be a real problem. Most gardeners reserve plastic pots for their moisture-loving plants.

Glazed pots, usually made of clay that is painted with a ceramic glaze, are also nonporous. Treat plants in glazed pots like those in plastic pots.

Pots without drainage present a problem. Once a plant is watered in an undrained pot, moisture remains in the potting mix until it is utilized or evaporated. Plants in drainless pots should receive less water than those in containers with drain holes. Just water a portion of the soil surface of these plants. A good rule-of-thumb is to add water equal to one-fourth of the total volume of the container. Watch these plants carefully for signs of improper watering.

One method of watering plants in pots without drainage is to insert a funnel into the soil with the funnel tip an inch under the soil surface. Pour water into the funnel until water no longer goes through it.

Plant differences. Plants that grow quickly and those that bloom or bear fruit heavily need more water than plants with a more conservative life style. Plants with a large total leaf surface, such as ferns, require more water than sparsely foliaged plants. Plants with soft, lush foliage need more water than those with waxy, leathery, or succulent leaves.

Does your plant need water?

Indoor gardeners use many different methods for judging when a plant needs to be watered. Experiment with various methods of testing moisture levels and then adapt the one you find most effective.

The touch test. Most indoor gardeners agree that this is the best method to judge a plant's need for water. Feel the soil surface with your finger. If the potting mix is dry to a depth of ½ to 1 inch, add water. If the potting mix is still moist, keep checking the plant periodically, as often as daily.

Drooping foliage. Drooping or wilted foliage on a house plant usually indicates it needs water fast! Water a wilted plant thoroughly; then wait. After several hours the plant should resume its normal appearance. House plants usually survive this wilting once or twice, but not indefinitely. Constantly wilting plants indicate poor gardening habits. For your plant's sake, don't rely on this method for judging water needs.

The weight test. Some people judge a potted plant's water needs by the weight of the pot. This is the rule-of-thumb: the lighter the pot, the less moisture present in the potting mix. To effectively judge the moisture present using this method, you must know what the pot and plant weigh both when well watered and when in need of water. This method is best left to the experienced gardener.

Tink . . . tunk! Some gardeners claim they can tell when a potted plant needs water by tapping the pot. If it sounds like "tunk," it doesn't require water; if it goes "tink," it needs water. To use this method, a good ear for "tinks" and "tunks" is necessary. The people who have it are probably the same ones who can tell a ripe watermelon by thumping it. This method also works best for an experienced gardener.

The water meter test. There are several new devices, generally called "electronic moisture meters," designed to measure the moisture present in your house plant's potting mix.

The meters all operate on a similar principle: they record the flow of a very weak electric current generated by a small battery or by a chemical reaction to moist soil. In most cases, the more moisture present in the soil, the stronger the flow of electric current. The meters then convert this current into a signal—a buzz, a click, a flashing light, or a visual scale or dial reading that tells you how moist the soil is.

To use such a meter, push the probe into the soil in the plant's container and wait for the signal. Try several readings on each plant at different soil depths to get an accurate idea of overall water content.

Water meters are available from nurseries, garden centers, and mail-order garden supply firms.

Whichever type of meter you purchase, follow the directions carefully and be alert for its shortcomings. You may get inaccurate readings if you water with distilled water or if there is a salt buildup in the potting mix. If your meter is battery operated, the battery could be weak or dead. So, should a house plant look wilted and have soil that appears bone dry, give it some water regardless of the water meter's message.

A good way to water

Provided your plant has the proper potting mix and drainage, proceed as follows: 1) Feel the top inch of the soil. If it is dry to the touch, add tepid water to the soil surface. 2) Continue to add water until you see it seeping from the drainage hole. 3) Allow the plant to drain (either into a sink or drainage tray) for a minimum of 10 minutes. 4) Discard any excess water standing in the tray (a potted plant should never sit in water). 5) Repeat this procedure when the soil surface again is dry to touch.

Use a watering can with a straight or slightly curved spout. This prevents you from spilling as you water.

After you have followed this watering procedure for a time, you should be able to estimate the amount of water your plants utilize. Add the amount of water each plant uses; then, in a few minutes, check the drainage trays for any excess water.

The soak

Many kinds of house plants, especially Boston ferns, benefit from occasionally having their entire pots immersed in water. Soak the pot (have water at room temperature) until bubbles stop coming to the surface; remove the plant and let it drain. Then return it to its normal place. Immediately after this periodic dunking is a good time to apply fertilizer. Fertilizing is discussed on pages 17-18.

The humidity factor

Most home atmospheres contain a negligible amount of humidity. To a few plant families, such as cactus and succulents, this lack of moisture in the air is no problem. The majority of plants we try to grow indoors, though, originated in tropical jungles, dripping with natural moisture. While a "rain forest" environment is hardly desirable for our homes, the responsibility falls to us to provide some of the humidity our tropical house plants require. Check the Plant Selection Guide (pages 26-79) to find the humidity needs of your individual plants.

Many factors affect the humidity level inside houses. During the winter months, heating systems reduce natural humidity. Warm summer temperatures also dispel most moisture. The humidity levels in your home can be gauged by a hygrometer, an instrument that measures moisture present in the air. Inexpensive hygrometers are usually available in hardware stores.

Several methods allow you to increase humidity for your plants: misting, utilizing humidity trays, grouping compatible plants, placing plants in naturally humid areas. These methods, used either individually or in combination, should benefit your moisture-loving plants.

Daily misting is an easy, inexpensive method of creating a humid atmosphere for your tropical plants. Opinions vary among indoor gardeners on the value of misting plants—daily misting is popular among many orchid and fern lovers; other gardeners mist only occasionally or not at all. Besides creating humidity, misting has the added advantage of cleaning foliage and discouraging pests.

Humidity trays: *They keep moisture-loving plants happy*

Two types of humidity trays you can create: (left) individual saucer filled with small pebbles holds plant so water level never touches pot; (right) large tray provides humidity for grouping of house plants.

Misting should create a fine spray of moisture that surrounds your plant and covers both sides of its leaves. Like watering, misting should be done in the morning so the moisture will have time to evaporate. It's best to let water sit in the mister overnight. Misting does not replace regular watering since the plant absorbs very little of the spray.

If your plant is situated where the spray might damage furniture or other interior surfaces, move the plant to a safe area for misting.

Some hairy-leafed plants, such as African violets, dislike being misted. Water drops on the leaves may cause spotting, especially if the water is below room temperature.

Plastic and metal misters are available in most nurseries or indoor plant stores. Be sure your mister sprays a fine mist; the plant leaves should look as if a light dew has settled on them, not be dripping wet.

Humidity trays provide for constant water evaporation around house plants. Waterproof trays, large enough to hold one plant or several, are filled with small rocks or pebbles. Add enough water to the tray so the water level remains just below the top of the rocks. The planted container rests on the rocks, preventing it from ever sitting in water (roots that sit constantly in water may rot). This tray will also catch any runoff created during regular watering.

Trays should be constructed of waterproof materials, such as metal, plastic, nonabsorbent rubber, or glazed ceramic. Clay saucers absorb and hold moisture that could damage tables, rugs, or other interior surfaces.

Some indoor gardeners create a "buffer zone" (see page 10) between their humidity trays and floor or furniture surfaces. This prevents any damage caused by condensation. Raising the tray a few inches from the surface forms an air layer to absorb any extra moisture.

To check the amount of humidity created by the tray method, use a hygrometer near the foliage.

Grouping compatible plants is another method of creating humidity indoors. All plants give off water vapor through their leaves in a process called transpiration (this process is described in more detail on pages 4-5). This water vapor creates humidity around each transpiring plant. Grouping plants together lets them share the created humidity.

Besides creating humidity for each other, a group of plants is always more interesting visually than the single parlor palm standing forlornly in a corner.

Naturally humid areas in most homes are the kitchen and the bathroom. The normal activities performed in these rooms, such as dishwashing, boiling water, or taking hot showers, create moisture in the air and frequently raise the humidity level.

Moisture-loving plants will thrive in these rooms if their other requirements, such as light and temperature, can also be met.

Fertilizing know-how

Many people think that adding fertilizer will feed their plants. This is not precisely true. Plants manufacture their own food by the process of photosynthesis. (Photosynthesis is discussed in detail on page 4.) The fertilizers you provide your house plants assist them in this food production. Most gardeners use the terms "fertilizing" and "feeding" interchangeably.

Plants growing in the ground outdoors can search for the nourishment they need. If their immediate area lacks needed nutrients, the roots can branch into outer areas. A house plant is confined to the soil in its pot; once the nutrients in the potting mix are gone, the plant is stranded. But you can replenish these nutrients by applying fertilizer.

House plant fertilizers usually contain three main nutrients: nitrogen, phosphorus, and potassium or potash. Some fertilizers also include needed trace elements. The ratio of these three ingredients is usually indicated on the label by three numbers, such as 5-10-5 or 18-20-16. The first number refers to nitrogen, which stimulates leaf growth and helps leaves maintain a rich green color. The second number indicates phosphorus, which promotes sturdy cell structure and healthy root growth and aids in flower and fruit production. The third number refers to potassium, which aids plants in normal plant functions and development. If you choose a fertilizer that indicates it is formulated for house plants, you can feel confident it is properly balanced in the three main nutrients.

Types of fertilizers

Commercial fertilizers for house plants come in several forms: liquids, powders, tablets, and capsules. Most of these fertilizers are to be dissolved and diluted in water for application. Some types are scratched into the soil surface. Tablets and slow-release capsules are also placed on the soil surface or in the soil. Slow-release fertilizers allow nutrients to be slowly dissolved in normal waterings over a period of time. Whichever type of house plant fertilizer you choose, read the label carefully and follow the directions exactly.

Using fertilizers

Many indoor gardeners find it very beneficial to apply fertilizers more frequently than normal (usually twice as often) but in a very diluted state (usually one-half the recommended dose or less). This provides the plant with nutrients in a more consistent manner.

Fertilizer requirements are given for many common house plants in the Plant Selection Guide on pages 26-79. Know your plant's needs before fertilizing.

Never apply fertilizer to dry potting mix. Be sure your plant has been thoroughly watered first.

A newly purchased house plant normally will have been well nourished at the nursery or greenhouse and will not need fertilizer for at least 3 months. A newly repotted plant will find sufficient nutrients in the new potting mix and won't need fertilizer for a while.

Never fertilize a sick plant. Wait until it has completely recovered before encouraging it to grow.

Most plants rest during the winter months. Don't coax them into growth by applying fertilizer. Most gardeners avoid fertilizers from about September to March. Don't add nutrients to dormant plants; wait until they show signs of growth.

Never deliberately overfertilize your plants. "An extra pinch to grow on" can damage a plant severely. If you find you have applied too much fertilizer, leaching your plant may wash out some of the excess. (Leaching means watering your plant so water comes out the drainage hole, letting it drain for a while, and then rewatering. Repeat this two or three times.)

Fertilizing through the leaves

Some indoor gardeners have found that spraying fertilizer on plant leaves is helpful to their plants.

Plants such as schefflera, philodendron, and Chinese evergreen respond positively—the leaves become a richer green, perhaps growing a bit.

Fertilize by spraying a fine mist of diluted fertilizer with a mister or atomizer until the leaves look as if a good dew has settled on them. Don't leave the foliage dripping wet.

All but the tenderest house plant can benefit from leaf feeding, but be careful not to overfertilize or feed too frequently. If your house plant fertilizer has no instructions for foliar feeding, use it at about half the recommended root feeding strength the first time. Increase the dosage to the full recommended strength in successive months.

Foliar feeding does not replace root feeding. Some gardeners root feed at the beginning of each month and then leaf feed at midmonth.

Pinching for size— pruning for shape

Plant size is an important consideration indoors. Limitations such as ceilings, table tops, and room size

Tip pinching: *The way to make plants bushy*

1. Leggy plant *needs to grow bushier, keep more compact form.*

2. Pinch out *growing tip of tallest stem; remove close to leaf joint.*

3. New growth *forms just below pinched-out tip, makes plant bushy.*

indicate the size your house plants should maintain. The solution to the problem of keeping plants to scale is careful pinching and pruning. Pinching encourages bushy growth, whereas pruning reshapes an overgrown plant. Root pruning, though somewhat more drastic, can increase the indoor life of a favorite plant.

One rule to remember: throw out or replace ugly plants. A house plant that has grown too leggy, unwieldy, or misshapen for restorative pruning no longer serves your purpose.

Tools for trimming

Though the average gardener requires a wide variety of pruning tools in all shapes and sizes, the indoor gardener needs only a few. The two most generally useful pruning tools are your thumb and forefinger— and these tools you'll never misplace. They can handle most pruning on soft-stemmed plants. Have a sharp knife, scissors, or hand pruners for tougher jobs.

Pinching

Like preventive medicine, proper use of the pinching technique avoids more drastic pruning measures. Pinching out the growing tip of a stem promotes side branching that creates thick, bushy plants; pinching stops growth in one direction and redirects it.

Using your thumb and forefinger, pinch out the top growth of a stem or branch. This forces side buds lower on the stem to form new branches. The resulting growth helps create a full, well-shaped plant and keeps it from becoming leggy. Tip pinching is shown at left.

Pinching should be used on fast-growing, branching plants—such as Swedish ivy, wandering Jew, or coleus—that can form new growth on pinched stems. Do not pinch a plant with a single growing stem, such as a dracaena or palm.

Repeat pinching as often as necessary during the plant's growing season. Be sure to pinch only stems that contain at least three or four sets of leaves; these are established and can support new growth.

Top pruning

Like pinching, top pruning restores the plant's desired shape. Removing leggy growth or branches grown awry improves the plant's appearance and, as with pinching, may encourage new growth.

Cut stems or branches back to where you want them. Use scissors or pruning shears if the stem is too stiff to be pinched off with thumb and forefinger. Always cut just above a leaf node or bud. Be sure to remove as much of the stem above the node as possible. The node or bud becomes the terminal growing point on the stem, and water and nutrients will travel no farther. The dead or dying stem is useless and could become diseased, endangering your plant.

If you decide to remove a whole branch, cut it off as close to the main stem as possible.

Root pruning

If a plant has reached the maximum size your house can accommodate, consider root pruning. This process takes courage but, if successful, permits your plant to remain in its present container. Root pruning techniques are illustrated below.

It's best to root prune a house plant during a time of active growth, usually in the spring. Have all materials ready so the procedure can be accomplished as quickly as possible. Remove the plant from its pot (see page 20 for instructions). With a sharp knife, trim off portions of the root ball on all sides. Cut quickly; do not saw or hack at roots. With plants that have fleshy roots, such as asparagus ferns, chlorophytum, syngonium, or dracaena, severe root pruning could be detrimental. Try washing all the old soil off the roots first. When the root-pruned plant is replaced in its container, there should be about a 1-inch clearance on all sides. Fill in

Root pruning: *One way to control plant size*

1. Remove plant *from pot. With sharp knife, slice off portions of root ball.*

2. Place root ball *on top of enough soil to bring plant up to pot rim.*

3. Top pruning *lets root-pruned plant recover; reshapes plant's appearance.*

the sides with new potting mix and tamp it in. Water the plant and return it to its place.

A root-pruned plant will revive more quickly if it is also top pruned.

When a plant outgrows its pot

Repotting gives house plants a new lease on life. It provides fresh potting mix, more root space to grow into, and a larger foundation for expanding foliage.

While the basic techniques for initial potting and for repotting (see pages 12-13) are the same, the purposes differ. Initial potting places a newly purchased plant in the container you prefer. Repotting releases an unhappy, potbound plant from a crowded environment and provides a new one.

The potbound plant is a prime candidate for repotting. Symptoms of this malady are roots growing out of the drainage hole, foliage appearing top-heavy in a too small pot, stunted growth, and water running quickly through the potting mix with little retention. Roots protruding from the drainage hole or an unbalanced appearance can easily be seen. To check on a watering problem, knock the plant out of its container and examine the root ball to see if the roots are damp, or the potting mix is soggy. Brown, mushy roots indicate a bad case of overwatering; remove all the wet potting mix and repot the plant in fresh mix.

To knock a plant out of its pot, brace the stem and soil surface with one hand and invert the pot with the other. Strike the pot rim carefully against a solid surface, such as a table top or counter; this should loosen the root ball and allow it to emerge in one piece. If the root ball refuses to budge after several thumps, run a sharp knife between the pot and root ball and invert the pot.

Once the root ball has been dislodged, examine it closely. If the ball shows mostly potting mix, replace the plant in its pot; being rootbound is not its problem. A root ball that shows mostly tangled roots and very little potting mix, though, needs to be repotted.

To repot your house plant, have all the needed supplies assembled. Quantities of the correct potting mix and the necessary tools should be handy. The new container should be ½ to 1 inch larger in diameter than the plant's present pot.

Be sure to keep the surface of the old root ball on top, filling in around the sides with new potting mix. Most plants adjust poorly to being buried.

Propagation pointers

Propagating their own house plants is a challenge that many indoor gardeners relish. New plants can be created in several ways, including stem and leaf cuttings, air layering, and divisions.

Some house plants—the piggyback (*Tolmiea menziesii*) and the spider plant (*Chlorophytum comosum*), for example—actually invite you to make new plants by providing you with tiny, conspicuous, easy-to-root plantlets.

You can get stem or leaf cuttings by pruning your own leggy or misshapen house plants, or you can find other enthusiastic indoor gardeners who are willing to share cuttings with you. Though you can't expect instant results with propagation, time and patience should reward you with many new house plants.

Rooting plantlets. These ready-made tiny plants appear as outgrowths or appendages above the soil on an established plant. The plantlet that forms at the base of a piggyback leaf (see page 76), develops on the bloomstalk of a spider plant (see page 33), or grows on the frond of a mother fern (see page 29) only needs to come in contact with moist potting mix to form roots and grow into a self-sufficient house plant.

The easiest method for rooting is to place the plantlet (still attached to the leaf or stalk of the parent plant) in a container filled with moist potting mix. Use hair pins or a partially opened paper clip, if necessary, to keep the plantlet in contact with the soil. Keep the mix constantly moist but not soggy. When you notice new growth on the plantlet, sever the connection with the parent plant by removing the stem. Or you can start by detaching the plantlet and placing it directly into the prepared soil.

Leaf and stem cuttings. Most cuttings will root in either potting mix or water. Prepare the cutting this way: remove lower leaves; dip the stem into rooting hormone and then insert it into the rooting medium. Keep the rooting medium moist but not soggy. When the cutting produces new growth, you can plant it.

For the rooting medium, you can use perlite, vermiculite, coarse sand, a mixture of half perlite/half sand, or a commercial potting mix with enough perlite added to make the mix lighter in texture. Whatever you choose, be sure it is sterilized to minimize the risk of disease organisms destroying the cutting before it can root. The procedures for rooting stem cuttings are illustrated on the next page.

Air layering. This propagation method is best for tall, lanky, single-stemmed plants—such as split-leaf philodendron (*Monstera deliciosa*)—that are difficult to grow from cuttings. The principle behind this method is simple: you cut or scar the stem to stimulate root formation at that point.

With a sharp knife or razor blade, cut or scar the plant stem just below a leaf node, cutting about halfway through the stalk. Brace the stem, if necessary, with a small piece of wood. Then place moist sphagnum around the cut stem, wrap it with clear plastic film, and tie the plastic in place. When roots begin to show through the plastic (this may take several weeks), sever the rooted portion from the parent and plant it. Air layering techniques are illustrated on the next page.

Divisions. With this propagation method, you create new plants by dividing the growing centers of large plants that grow in clumps or form multiple growing centers. Each clump or crown—called a growth center —has its own root system. Agapanthus, asparagus ferns, and African violets can be propagated in this way.

All you need to do is remove the parent plant from its container, brush or wash away the potting mix around the roots, and carefully cut or pull apart the various growth centers. Then repot each of the individual plants into smaller containers.

Air layering: *Cutting an overgrown plant down to size*

1. Brace *stem and cut a notch half-way through stem with a sharp knife.*

2. Wrap *moistened sphagnum moss around notched portion of plant stem.*

3. Secure *moss (to stem) with a piece of plastic tied in place at top, bottom.*

Stem cuttings: *Many plants from a single parent*

1. Cut *stem off just above leaf node; make sure cutting has several leaves.*

2. Remove *two or three lower leaves from cutting to expose stem.*

3. Dip *prepared stem into rooting hormone powder; knock off any excess.*

4. Use *a pencil to prepare a hole in rooting medium for stem cutting.*

5. Place *cutting into hole carefully. Don't force it into position.*

6. Tamp *cutting into place with fingers; then moisten rooting medium.*

If your plant has problems...

While dusting leaves, *indoor gardener can examine plant for any possible leaf damage, pests, plant diseases.*

Is your plant sick or unhappy? Brown leaf tips, stunted or abnormal growth, leaves turning yellow and falling off, wilting—these signs and many others signal a plant problem. The culprits can be pests, plant diseases, or, most likely, improper care.

The following chapter gives you guidelines for diagnosing your house plant's problems and corrective measures for solving those problems. One thing you should keep in mind: some plants will be too far gone to be restored to their former appearances. The best approach to these plants is to steel yourself to discard them. There is nothing attractive or appealing about a sickly plant, and its problem might spread to its companions.

Prevent trouble before it happens

Though no indoor plant is immune to problems, pests, or plant diseases, taking simple precautions will reduce the chance of its experiencing a setback in development. Most of the following preventive measures are discussed elsewhere in this book, but they are worth repeating:

1) Always use clean plant containers and sterilized potting mix when planting or transplanting to give your house plants a fresh start.

2) Carefully examine plants before bringing them home to be sure they are free of pests and diseases.

3) Isolate new house plants for a few weeks (if you have adequate space) to be sure they are healthy and free of pests and diseases before adding them to your plant collection.

4) Look up each house plant in the Plant Selection Guide on pages 26-79 to study its growing requirements. (Most common house plants are listed in this guide.) Try to provide your plant with as many of its needs as possible.

5) Develop the habit of routine inspection as described on pages 14-15.

6) If you find a sick plant in your home, isolate it from other house plants until it is cured. This helps prevent pests or disease from spreading.

Common plant problems

Most house plant problems you find will be the result of improper care. And, as with most problems, the cause is rarely a simple one. Poor indoor gardening habits, a bad growing location, or a combination of the two can cause various reactions in your plant's appearance. Treat these reactions as a call for help; left without aid, your house plant will die.

This section lists plant problems by the effect each problem has on a plant's appearance, offers possible causes, and suggests methods for correction. Study each plant's problem carefully; try to diagnose and treat it as quickly as possible. If you are unsure of how to correct a problem, refer to the appropriate section of this book.

Leaf tips and leaf margins turn brown from improper plant care. Overwatering or underwatering, too much sun or heat through a window, too much fertilizer, watering with a water high in salt concentration, not enough humidity, locating the plant in drafts, or a combination of these care problems may result in browned tips or margins. Study your plant's situation and try to locate the possible cause. Then remedy it. If the cause isn't easily discernible, try eliminating each possibility, one at a time.

Yellowing leaves on house plants have a variety of possible causes. Not enough light or too much light and lack of fertilizer or too much fertilizer are common problems. Yellowing leaves may also be the result of a high nighttime temperature or too much water. Sucking insects (probably scale insects or mealybugs) on plant stems between the yellowing leaves and the roots are another possible cause. Study the care you give your plant to locate the cause of the yellowing foliage. The green color may or may not return to the damaged leaves after the problem is corrected.

Leaf drop can be caused by one problem or a combination of several. Overwatering or underwatering, too much sun, too much fertilizer, not enough humidity, or a drafty location can cause leaves to drop. If only the lower leaves drop, your plant probably needs more light. Once leaves have fallen off because of improper care, they seldom grow back. However, you can save the plant by correcting the cause of the problem.

Wilting is a normal plant reaction to too much sun or heat, too much or not enough water, or a poor growing location. Try moving the plant to a better spot and check your watering techniques. Plants that need water will perk up quickly from a needed drink. This process isn't detrimental to the plant as long as it isn't allowed to wilt too frequently.

Dry and brittle leaves may mean your plant isn't getting enough water or the humidity levels are too low. Review your watering practices. Try regular misting or place the plant on a humidity tray (humidity trays are discussed on page 17).

Leggy growth is caused by insufficient light. Try moving your house plant to a location with more light and pinch back the leggy stems.

Brown or yellow spots on leaf edges or surfaces are unsightly and indicate too much water, too much direct sun, or a drafty location. Check the plant's present situation and make the needed corrections.

No flowers on a normally flowering house plant may be caused by a variety of conditions. Not enough light or

room temperatures that remain too high at night are possible causes. Try moving your blooming plant to a well-lighted spot. Check the nighttime temperature of its new location; if the temperature is too high, find a well-lighted, cool spot or move the plant every evening to a cool area.

Flower buds drop off for many reasons. Possible causes are inadequate light or too much sun, low room temperature, improper watering habits, or not enough fertilizer. Check your house plant's individual situation to pinpoint the problem.

Soft stem bases on house plants usually indicate rot. Overwatering is probably the culprit. Watch your watering habits carefully.

Soggy soil is the result of overwatering and/or improper drainage. Knock out the root ball (see page 20) to check the drainage problem; make sure the drainage hole isn't plugged. If overwatering created the problem, try to restrain that heavy hand when it's time to water.

Know your pests

Indoor pests are small, sometimes almost microscopic. You may not be aware of the little creatures until your favorite plant takes a turn for the worse. The routine inspection, discussed on pages 14-15, should nip most pest problems in the bud. If you do find pests, eradicate them as quickly as possible. Plants do not always recover even if all the pests are destroyed.

There are two approaches to pest control: one is direct, involving physical removal of the pests; the other requires using pesticides, which is less direct and not always beneficial to the plant.

The direct approach is to remove pests by hand or to wash them off with water from a hose or under a water faucet. Some gardeners have been successful using a mist sprayer. An advantage this approach of-

Washing plants *off is easy in a sink with sprayer hose attachment. Force of water removes dust, any pests.*

fers is that it can be repeated as often as needed to control pests. Most insecticides require a certain waiting period between doses. The chief problem with this method is that you might miss eliminating insect eggs in the soil.

Spraying plants with insecticides can be almost as harmful to some house plants as the pest infestation itself. Always read and carefully follow the directions on the label of all pesticides. Be sure the insecticide will effectively eliminate the specific pest attacking your plant and that it is recommended for use on house plants. If you use a spray specifically formulated for house plants, be sure it is recommended for use on your particular plant. Some tender plants, such as ferns, may succumb to the spray itself. It's best to spray plants outdoors. When you do, any spray residue will be dispersed outside in the open air, and you can be sure to cover the leaf surfaces, both top and bottom, without worrying about damaging furniture surfaces. The push-button containers of house plant insecticides are best for the indoor gardener, both in ease and economy. Other types of sprays need to be mixed, a time-consuming and messy process that requires special equipment, and these insecticides are available only in large quantities.

Your first step is to identify your plant problem as a pest infestation. Some pests, such as mealybugs or aphids, will be visible on the plant or in the container; others, too small for visual identification, can also cause extensive plant damage. Once you've determined a pest problem, isolate the infected plant immediately to prevent infection of other plants. The following section contains information on identifying each house plant pest, the plant damage the pests create, and the various methods of eliminating them.

Aphids

Aphids have soft, round or pear-shaped bodies, usually green, reddish, or black. They may have wings. They tend to cluster on buds or on new plant growth.

Plant damage. Aphids suck plant juices, causing poor growth, stunted plants, or curled, distorted leaves or flowers. Their honeydew secretions give leaves a shiny appearance and may form a base for the growth of a sooty mold.

Control. Wash aphids off with water from a hose, with a mist sprayer, or in a soapy (*not* detergent) solution. Pyrethrum or rotenone can also be used.

Mealybugs

Though large enough to be spotted easily, mealybugs normally cluster on leaf stems or in branch crotches out of the light, making them difficult to detect. They have round, white, fuzzy-looking bodies.

Plant damage. Mealybugs — sucking insects — cause stunted growth, eventually killing house plants. They also secrete a honeydew that gives leaves a shiny, sticky surface and forms a base on which black mold can grow.

Control. Remove mealybugs by touching them with a cotton swab dipped in alcohol, washing them off with water from a hose or a spray mister, or spraying them with petroleum oils.

Scale insects

Scale exists in many varieties. Usually brown or gray with a round or oval-shaped body, scale insects have a hard-shell covering in their adult stage. Some types attack plant leaves; others attack stems. They can be especially difficult to detect on fern fronds because they resemble spores.

Plant damage. Scales are sucking insects that use plant juices for food. They cause stunted or poor plant growth. They also secrete honeydew that gives leaves a shiny, sticky surface and forms a base for the growth of sooty mold.

Control. Scrape off scale insects with your fingernail or with a small knife or wash them off in a soapy (*not* detergent) water solution. Lime sulfur or petroleum oils are also effective in controlling scale for some plants; read the container label.

Spider mites

A common house plant pest, the spider mite is so small that it is detectable only in groups or by the characteristic webbing it leaves on plant foliage. Mites have flat, oval bodies, usually white or red.

Plant damage. Leaves may yellow and die or fall off. Some leaves become mottled with brown or yellow spots. Leaf undersides are covered with a fine webbing. Infected plants become stunted and may die.

Control. Isolate infested plants at once. Spider mites spread like wildfire. Wash off with water from a hose or in a soapy (*not* detergent) solution. Lime sulfur, dusting sulfur, or petroleum oils are effective, too. Regular misting also helps to control mites.

Thrips

Very small and fast-moving thrips are barely visible. They have slender bodies in colors of tan, browns, or black, with lighter-colored markings. When disturbed, they may fly or leap.

Plant damage. Thrips feed on foliage or flowers, causing distorted growth of the plant tissue. Their rasping damage is sometimes visible on stems or leaf edges.

Control. Wash thrips off with water from a hose or with a mist sprayer. Apply pyrethrum, rotenone, or petroleum oils.

Whiteflies

These common pests, found both indoors and out, are very small and have white bodies and wings. They flutter about plants in a white cloud when the plant they're attacking is disturbed. The young attach themselves to the underside of leaves.

Plant damage. Attacked leaves turn a pale color. The foliage surface is covered with a shiny, sticky layer of honeydew. The honeydew forms a base on which sooty mold can grow.

Control. Wash whiteflies off with water from a hose or with a mist sprayer. Apply pyrethrum, rotenone, or petroleum oil to the infested plant. Several applications may be necessary.

Plant diseases

For house plants to develop diseases is rather uncommon. Most disease problems result from poor growing conditions, improper care, or purchasing an already diseased plant. Carefully examine a plant for signs of disease before purchasing it; guidelines are given on page 7.

Crown or root rot is usually caused by poor drainage and overwatering. Plants may turn brown or suddenly wilt. If the plant isn't too far gone, transplanting may be beneficial. Correcting your watering habits should avoid a recurrence of this disease.

Mildew appears on plant leaves, stems, or flower buds as a white or gray powder. Leaves may curl or be distorted. Overwatering and poor air circulation are probable causes. Try moving the infected plant to a better location, correct your watering habits, and, if necessary, spray the infected house plant with sulfur dust or benomyl.

Plant selection guide

This comprehensive guide offers you a list of common plants that can be successfully grown indoors. The plants described as "indoor-outdoor plants" can be brought indoors periodically to be enjoyed, but they are primarily suited to be grown outdoors.

To better help you locate and identify them, many of these house plants are pictured. Most of the plants listed can be found in containers of various sizes in nurseries, indoor plant boutiques, or florist shops.

Plants are listed alphabetically by their botanical names. Common name listings will direct you to the botanical name listing that gives you a description of the plant's appearance and growth habits, its care requirements, and other related varieties that also make suitable house plants.

ABUTILON. Flowering maple, Chinese lantern. Tropical plant from South America grown for its globe-shaped flowers that can bloom the year around. Pinch constantly to control growth and extend bloom. Can be grown upright or trained to hang. Needs at least 4 hours full sun daily and likes regular fertilizing and potting mix kept moist. See photo on page 50.

A. megapotamicum

A. hybridum. Bell-shaped flowers come in white, pink, yellow, and red. The best-known flowering maple.

A. megapotamicum. Weeping Chinese lantern. Drooping growth good for baskets. Flowers red and yellow.

A. striatum thompsonii. Variegated foliage, green with creamy yellow; flowers are orange veined with red.

ACALYPHA hispida. Chenille plant, Red-hot cattail. Nicknames come from long, tassel-like red or purple blooms. Has bright green, hairy leaves. Needs heavy pruning to control size. Provide bright light, humidity; keep potting mix moist but not soggy. *Acalypha* hates wet feet. Fertilize during growing season. Use standard potting mix.

Buying a plant? *Be a wise shopper; know type of house plant you want and growing conditions it will require.*

ACHIMENES. Tropical American plant that grows from rhizomes. Best used in hanging baskets. Flowers in blue, pink, yellow, red, purple. Needs bright light (no direct sun), temperatures above 60°, potting mix kept evenly moist during growing season. Fertilize dur

ing blooming season. To grow: Plant rhizomes March-April, placing ½-1 inch deep in moist peat moss and sand. Keep in light shade at 60° with constant moisture. When growth is 3 inches, plant in standard potting mix. In fall, dry rhizomes and let soil dry out; store in cool dry spot; repot in spring and resume watering.

ADIANTUM raddianum (*A. cuneatum*). Maidenhair fern. Wiry, black stems hold lacy, bright green, fan-shaped leaflets. Plants need potting mix high in organic matter, shade (north or sunless window), steady moisture (never let roots dry out), good drainage, high humidity (likes mist

ing), cool temperatures preferably below 65°. Mature fronds die back but new ones soon appear. Cut out dead fronds for appearance. Can be moved outdoors to a shaded patio for summer. Is considered difficult.

AECHMEA. Bromeliad that grows in the vase form. Plant in a fast-draining but moisture-retentive potting mix. Likes bright light (no hot sun), regular fertilizing. Water when soil is really dry to touch; fill vase with water. Divide when new plant forms at base. See photo on page 67.

A. fasciata

A. chantinii. Olive to brownish green leaves barred with silver. Flower cluster has yellow blooms; orange, red, or pink bracts tipped yellow and white.

A. fasciata. Green leaves banded white with a powdery surface. Flower cluster begins blue, changes to deep rose with age. Bracts are pink.

A. 'Foster's Favorite'. Wine red, lacquered leaves. Flowers on drooping, spikelike clusters in coral red and blue.

A. fulgens discolor. Green leaves backed with purple. Flowers are red tipped in blue; berries follow.

A. 'Royal Wine'. Dark green leaves backed with dark wine color. Flowers deep orange tipped in blue.

AEONIUM. Decorative succulent with leaves in rosettes. Likes good light, air circulation. Water when potting mix feels dry to touch. (Be sure roots dry out.) Plant in ½ standard potting mix, ½ sharp sand. Propagate from leaf or stem cuttings. See photo on page. 79.

A. canariense

A. arboreum atropurpureum. Dark maroon leaves.

A. canariense. Apple green leaves.

A. swartzkopf. Black leaves.

AERIDES. Epiphytic orchids from tropical Asia that can become quite tall. Plants have central stem with fleshy green leaves. Flower spikes hold closely set, fragrant, waxy flowers in summer. Likes bright

A. multiflorum

light, humidity. Needs ample water spring, summer; less the rest of year.

A. crassifolium. To 10 inches; amethyst purple flowers.

A. multiflorum. White and purple summer flowers.

A. odoratum. To 40 inches; 1-inch flowers are white mottled with purple. Spicy fragrance.

AESCHYNANTHUS (Trichosporum). Basket vine. Shining leaves usually in pairs on drooping stems; good in hanging baskets. Tubular flowers. Prefers warm temperatures, high humidity, regular fertilizing, good light. Keep pot

A. lobbianus

ting mix moist but not soggy. Plant in loose, open, fibrous potting mix. Use stem cuttings to propagate.

A. lobbianus. Lipstick vine. Red, 2-inch tubular flowers emerge from calyces like lipsticks from cases.

A. marmoratus. Zebra basket vine. Green foliage mottled with maroon. Green tubular flowers.

A. speciosus. Yellow and orange flowers up to 4 inches long.

African violet. See Saintpaulia ionantha.

AGAPANTHUS. Lily-of-the-Nile. Large container plant that can summer outdoors. Grow evergreen varieties in sunny window in standard potting mix. Likes lots of water during growing season. Keep potbound for good bloom. Divide when plant outgrows container.

A. africanus

A. africanus (often sold as *A. umbellatus*). Evergreen. Most common variety. Flower stalks to 1½ feet. Blue or white flowers midsummer to fall.

A. 'Dwarf White'. Evergreen. Foliage to 1-1½ feet. White flowers on stalks 1½-2 feet tall.

A. 'Peter Pan'. Evergreen dwarf variety. Foliage 8-12 inches tall. Blue flowers on 12-18-inch stems.

AGAVE. Century plant. Use smaller varieties indoors. Succulent that prefers a sunny window, warm temperatures; let potting mix dry out completely between waterings. Plant in ½ standard potting mix, ½ sharp sand. Fertilize infrequently to keep compact. Divide new plants that form near base.

A. picta

A. filifera. Thread Agave. Narrow, olive green leaves with loose, curled threads at margins.

A. picta. Narrow, pale green leaves with white margins, small black teeth.

A. victoriae-reginae. Olive green leaves, white lines.

AGLAONEMA. Hardy tropical with graceful oblong leaves, variegated on some types. Likes standard potting mix, warm temperatures, good light, frequent waterings, but adaptable to poor light and low moisture. Great for poorly lighted situations. Small greenish flowers resemble callas. Cuttings will grow a long time in plain water. Exudation from leaf tips, especially from *A. modestum,* spots wood finishes. Propagate by stem cuttings. See photo on page 34.

A. modestum

A. commutatum. Deep green leaves with pale green markings. Variety 'White Rajah' has white markings.

A. modestum. Chinese evergreen. Shiny, dark green leaves.

A. roebelinii. Leathery leaves marked with pale green.

A. treubii. Bluish green leaves marked with silver. Plant grows to 10 inches.

ALOE. Easy-to-grow succulent of the lily family, mostly from South Africa. Forms clumps of fleshy, pointed leaves with clusters of orange, yellow, or red flowers. Plant in well-drained soil; likes a sunny window, can tolerate less. Let soil dry between waterings; be sure to soak plants thoroughly. Divide into clumps to propagate.

A. variegata

A. nobilis. Pointed, dark green leaves edged with irregular white teeth; rosette form on a short stem. Flowers orange red.

A. striata. Coral aloe. Stiff pointed leaves, gray green with narrow pinkish edge; rosette form on short stem.

A. variegata. Tiger aloe. Wavy bands of white markings on green leaves. Flowers pink to dull red.

A. vera. Pale green leaves with hard spines, upright growth to 12 inches. Sap used medicinally as a home remedy for burns.

Aluminum plant. See Pilea cadierei.

ANANAS. Pineapple. Bromeliad that may bear fruit indoors. Can be grown from leafy top of commercial pineapple: cut off top, remove any flesh, and let dry for a week in a shady spot; peel off any dried lower leaves and plant. Likes standard potting mix, good light, temperatures above 68°. Water when soil feels dry. Fertilize every 3-4 weeks.

A. nanas

A. comosus. Stiff, spiny, dark green leaves; produces edible fruit.

A. nanas. Most common pineapple. Gray green leaves. Produces fruit.

Angel's tears. See Soleirolia soleirolii.

ANTHURIUM. Exotic perennial native to tropical America. Shiny, dark green leaves with lustrous flower bracts in red, pink, white. No more difficult to grow indoors than some orchids. Likes high humidity, 50 percent or above. Keep plants on humidity trays; mist leaves several times daily. Give good light but not direct sun.

Grows best in 80°-90° temperatures but adaptable to less; growth stops if temperature drops below 65°. Keep out of drafts. Plant in a coarse, porous mix of leaf mold, sandy soil, and shredded osmunda. Give ample water at room temperature. Fertilize with a mild feeding every 4 weeks.

APHELANDRA squarrosa. Native to Mexico, South America. Showy, dark green, waxy leaves with white veins; large yellow flower clusters. Requires diffused light or morning sun, standard potting mix, 50°-70° temperatures, high humidity; routine watering. Prune plants to keep compact. To make plants bushy, cut stems back to 1 or 2 pair of leaves after flowering. Use stem cuttings to propagate.

A. s. 'Louisae'

A. s. 'Brockfeld'. Grows compactly with broader leaves than 'Louisae'. Leaves glossy black with straw yellow veining.

A. s. 'Dania'. Most compact in growth.

A. s. 'Louisae'. Best-known variety.

Aralia elegantissima. See Dizygotheca elegantissima.

ARAUCARIA heterophylla. *(A. excelsa).* Norfolk Island pine. Slow-growing evergreen with pyramidal form; can reach 12 feet indoors. Branches grow in tiers. Can be kept in container for many years; can double as indoor Christmas tree. May be summered outdoors; keep out of hot sun. Likes cool temperatures, good light, standard potting mix. Don't crowd; needs good air circulation. Needs lots of water, good drainage.

Arrowhead plant. See Syngonium podophyllum.

Artillery plant. See Pilea microphylla.

ASPARAGUS, ORNAMENTAL. Asparagus fern. Not a true fern but has the same feathery qualities. Fast grower. Thrives in standard potting mix with peat moss or ground bark added. Provide adequate drainage. Likes good light, ample water; can tolerate less. Leaves will turn yellow in inadequate light.

A. densiflorus 'Myeri'

Does not require as much humidity as true fern but likes frequent misting. Red spider mites common pests. To propagate, divide large plants. See photos on pages 55 and 74.

A. asparagoides 'Myrtifolius'. Baby smilax. Has broad glossy "leaves." Can be a hanger.

A. densiflorus 'Myeri' *(A. meyeri).* Plume asparagus, Foxtail asparagus. Stiff, upright stems densely covered with tiny needles.

A. d. 'Sprengeri' *(A. sprengeri).* Sprenger asparagus. Most common variety. Hardy grower with drooping stems. Good as a hanger. Mature form has tiny, pinkish flowers followed by coral red berries.

A. retrofractus. Ming fern. Erect, shrubby. Slender zigzag, silvery gray stems; threadlike leaves in fluffy, rich green tufts. Clusters of small white flowers.

A. setaceus *(A. plumosus).* Hardy plant with delicate feathery appearance. Dark green foliage. Commonly used by florists as fillers in bouquets.

ARCHONTO-PHOENIX cunninghamiana *(Seaforthia elegans).* Palm native to Australia has single trunk. Stately plant spreads up to 15 feet. Likes average house conditions, bright light (can tolerate shade).

Let potting mix dry out between waterings. Large plants may be difficult to transplant. See photo on page 63.

ASPIDISTRA elatior *(A. lurida).* Cast-iron plant. Sturdy, long-lived foliage plant with a strong constitution. Tough, glossy, dark green leaves, 1-2½ feet long, 3-4 inches wide. Though tolerant of a variety of conditions, prefers high humidity, cool temperatures, standard potting mix kept constantly moist, and fertilizing in spring and summer. Light can range from dark shade to filtered sun. See photo on page 39.

ASPLENIUM. Spleenwort. Widespread, variable group of graceful, hardy ferns. Plant in standard potting mix and give lots of water. Be sure drainage is good. Likes high humidity (use humidity trays), good sunless light as in north window. Plants may turn brown in winter if humidity is excessive.

A. nidus

See photos on page 71 and back cover.

A. bulbiferum. Mother fern, Mother spleenwort. Native to Malaysia, New Zealand. Upward growth of feathery, bright green fronds may reach 4 feet. Forms tiny new plantlets on fronds that can be removed and planted. Likes frequent misting.

A. nidus. Bird's-nest fern. Showy, apple green, undivided fronds with black rib unfurl from heart of plant. Can be summered outdoors on a shady patio. Water accumulation in heart may cause crown rot. Fronds dislike being touched.

ASTROPHYTUM. Cactus native to Mexico. Likes warm temperatures, good air circulation. Plant in equal parts standard potting mix and sharp sand. Water when potting mix dries out completely. See photo on page 79.

A. myriostigma

A. capricorne. Goat's horn. Green globe with silver markings. Yellow, 3-inch flowers with red throats.

A. myriostigma. Bishop's cap. Gray-ribbed, spineless globe; yellow flowers.

Baby tears. See Pilea depressa, Soleirolia soleirolii.

Bamburanta. See Ctenanthe compressa.

BAMBUSA multiplex riviereorum. Chinese goddess bamboo. Indoor-outdoor plant. Graceful, dense clump growth to 4-6 feet. Needs wide space to show off properly. Not recommended for year-round indoor culture but can spend extended periods indoors in containers. Give cool temperatures, bright light. To restrain growth, keep potting mix on the dry side. Fertilize regularly and re-pot every 2-3 years. When moving indoors or out, avoid sudden changes.

Banana. See Musa.

Bear's foot fern. See Humata tyermannii.

BEAUCARNEA recurvata *(Nolina)*. Elephant-foot tree, Pony tail. Hardy, palmlike. Grows vigorously indoors. Only barrier is ceiling height. Move outdoors when too large. A conversation piece, palm has bulbous trunk base resembling an elephant's foot. Crown of leaves tops trunk. Likes warm, dry atmosphere. Water only when potting mix completely dry. See photo on page 43.

BEGONIA. A huge group of plants, most of which make superb house plants. Generally prefer filtered light, regular fertilizing, rich potting mix that is slightly acid (add peat moss, leaf mold, or organic matter to standard potting mix). Keep plants constantly moist with perfect drainage. Following is a partial list of

B. rex-cultorum

terms and plant kinds you may encounter. Propagate by leaf or stem cuttings. See photos on pages 42 and 75.

Angel-wing begonias. Cane-stemmed begonias with pairs of leaves that resemble extended wings.

B. 'Corallina de Lucerna' ('Lucerna'). Angel-wing. Leaves are silver spotted. Clusters of coral flowers. Likes strong light but not hot sun. Keep soil constantly moist. Prune hard after flowering to keep bushy.

B. 'Erythrophylla' *(B. 'Feastii')*. Beefsteak begonia. Rhizomatous. Round, 2-3-inch leaves, dark green top, deep red below. Pink flowers.

B. fuchsioides. Fibrous-rooted. Small, bright green, shiny leaves; drooping clusters of pink or red flowers.

B. masoniana. Iron cross begonia. Rhizomatous. Big, rough, chartreuse green leaves centered with a brown marking that resembles a Maltese or German cross. Insignificant white flowers with dark bristles.

B. rex-cultorum. Rex begonia. Many varieties with magnificently colored, shieldlike leaves. Leaf colors in maroon, lilac, rose, greens, silvery gray, and combinations. Don't overfeed or overwater. Give good light, no hot sun. May go dormant in winter.

B. semperflorens. Wax begonia. Fibrous-rooted dwarf (4-6 inches), best indoors. Leaves bright green, bronzy, or reddish, some with reddish ribs. Flowers, single or double, in white, red, rose, pinks. Can take sun if well watered. Calla lily begonias are a kind of *B. semperflorens* with some foliage variegated with white. Rather delicate. Give cool temperatures, bright light (no hot sun), high humidity. Avoid overwatering.

Cane-stemmed begonias. Fibrous-rooted begonias whose stems have bamboolike joints. Growth erect or spreading. Includes angel-wing begonias.

Elatior begonias. Recently introduced. Winter blooming with single red, red orange, and pink on upright plants; double red, rose, pink flowers on sprawling plants. Like good light but not hot sun. Water when top inch of potting mix is dry to touch. Keep water off leaves to prevent mildew. Fertilize sparingly for good bloom. Summer bloom can be forced by putting plant in dark room to create longer nights.

Fibrous-rooted begonias. Begonias that grow from masses of fibrous roots. Mostly easy to grow.

Rhizomatous begonias. Begonias that form a rhizome (a thick, short stem, usually creeping, sometimes underground). Don't overfeed or overwater; the rhizome serves as a sort of emergency canteen that sustains plants through adversity. Give good light, no hot sun. May go dormant in winter; keep on the dry side until new growth resumes.

BELOPERONE guttata. Shrimp plant. Native to Mexico. Indoor-outdoor plant. Apple green, oval leaves; tubular flowers are white, purple-spotted, enclosed in copper bronze, with overlapping bracts resembling large shrimp. Constant pinching needed to keep plant bushy, compact. Likes at least 4 hours of sun daily (outdoors in summer, grow in partial shade; bracts and foliage fade in too much sun), standard potting mix, regular fertilizing, high humidity. Water when soil surface is almost dry; too much or too little water may cause leaf drop. Use stem cuttings to propagate.

BILLBERGIA. Epiphytic bromeliad native to Brazil. Stiff, spiny-toothed leaves in rosette form. Long-lasting tubular flowers on long, arching stems. Plant in equal parts sharp sand and fir bark or leaf mold. Likes bright light (can take morning sun), regular fertilizing, warm temperatures. Mist frequently. Keep vase at center of leaf rosette filled with water. Needs lots of water

B. nutans

during growth, much less in winter. Divide when offshoots form.

B. nutans. Queen's tears. Leaves green with silver cast. Flowers chartreuse green tipped in violet red; bracts rose red.

B. pyramidalis. Large plant. Leaves to 3 feet long. Flowers red, violet-tipped; red bracts.

Bird of paradise. See Strelitzia reginae.

Bird's-nest fern. See Asplenium nidus.

Blood-leaf. See Iresine herbstii.

Boston fern. See Nephrolepis exaltata 'Bostoniense'.

BRASSAIA actinophylla *(Schefflera actinophylla).* Queensland umbrella tree, Octopus tree, Umbrella plant. Shiny, oval, pointed leaves; 7-16 leaflets held on long stems; leaves radiate outward like umbrella ribs. Can become large. Needs room to show form. Likes standard potting mix, occasional fertilizing, bright light; plants can tolerate adverse conditions. Let potting mix dry completely between waterings. Frequent misting keeps leaves clean, discourages pests.

BROMELIAD. Any plant that belongs to the bromelia or pineapple family *(Bromeliaceae).* Most bromeliads are stemless perennials with clustered leaves and with showy flowers in simple or branched clusters with colorful bracts. Leaves of many kinds are handsomely marked. Most kinds grown indoors are epiphytes, plants that perch in trees or rocks and gain their sustenance from rain and leaf mold gathering around their roots. These often have cupped leaf bases or "vases" that hold water between rains. For bromeliads that will grow indoors, see *Aechmea, Ananas, Billbergia, Cryptanthus zonatus, Dyckia fosteriana, Guzmania lingulata, Neoregelia, Nidularium innocentii, Tillandsia lindeniana, Vriesia.*

Butterfly orchid. See Oncidium.

Button fern. See Pellaea rotundifolia.

CACTUS. Large family of succulent plants (see Succulents, page 76). Generally leafless, with stems modified into cylinders, pads, or joints that store water in times of drought. Their thick skin reduces evaporation, and most species have spines to protect plants against browsing animals. Flowers are usually large and brightly colored; fruits may be colorful, and a few are edible. All (with one doubtful exception) are native to the Americas. Many are native to drier parts of the West: these like fast-draining potting mix, at least 4 hours of sun daily, watering when the soil dries out completely, fertilizing in spring and summer, and a dormant period during winter (give less water, no fertilizer). Some are jungle cactus that grow as epiphytes in trees (like some orchids): these need rich potting mix with good drainage, frequent watering and fertilizing, filtered light. For cactus that can be used as house plants, see *Astrophytum, Cephalocereus, Chamaecereus silvestri, Echinocactus grusonii, Echinocereus, Echinopsis, Epiphyllum, Gymnocalycium, Lobivia, Mammillaria, Notocactus, Opuntia, Schlumbergera.*

CALADIUM bicolor. Fancy-leafed caladium. Native to tropical America. Grows from tubers. Brightly colored, arrow-shaped, translucent leaves in red, pink, white, green, and silver, often with a variety of colors on the same leaf. Likes good filtered light, warm temperatures (at least 70° in daytime), high humidity. Keep potting mix constantly moist during grow-

ing season. Start tubers in March. Pot in equal parts coarse sand and leaf mold, ground bark, or peat moss. Use 5-inch pot for 2½-inch tubers; 7-inch pot for 1 larger or 2 smaller tubers. Fill pot half full with mix; stir in 1 heaping teaspoon fish meal. Add 1 inch mix; set tuber in with knobby side up; cover with 2 inches mix. Water thoroughly. Keep soil constantly moist as leaves develop. Mist frequently. Feed with liquid fish fertilizer once a week, starting when leaves appear. Gradually withhold water when leaves start to die down. In about a month, lift tubers, remove most of soil, dry for 10 days. For winter, store in peat moss or vermiculite at temperatures between 50°-60°.

CALATHEA. Striking foliage plant native to tropical America, Africa. Usually called *Maranta* (see page 56), to which it is closely related. Foliage beautifully marked in shades of green, white, and pink. Requires high humidity, filtered sun (good light necessary for rich leaf color), standard potting mix, warm temperatures (above 55°). Mist frequently. Keep potting mix constantly moist but never soggy; stagnant conditions are harm-

C. makoyana

ful. Repot as often as necessary to avoid rootbound condition. See photo on page 47.

C. insignis. Rattlesnake plant. Long (12-18 inches), yellow green leaves striped olive green.

C. makoyana. Peacock plant. Leaves with areas of olive green or cream above, pink blotches below.

C. ornata. Sturdy. Leaves rich green above, purplish red below. Juvenile leaves pink-striped between veins.

C. zebrina. Zebra plant. Compact growth. Long velvety green with alternating bars of pale yellow green and olive green extending outward from midrib; purplish red underneath.

CALLISIA elegans. Striped inch plant. Native to Mexico. A creeper with white or yellow-striped green leaves with purple underneath. Related to *Tradescantia* (page 76) and *Zebrina* (page 77). Good for hanging containers. Grows best in filtered light, average house temperatures, standard potting mix. Check moisture level frequently (even daily); *Callisia* likes lots of water. Frequent pinching will promote compact growth.

CAPSICUM annuum. An ornamental pepper. Usually a colorful Christmas gift plant. Annual; may be grown from seed. Spring white flowers followed by colorful red fruit in fall. Likes at least 4 hours of sun daily, standard potting mix, cool temperatures, ample water.

Carrion flowers. See Stapelia.

CARYOTA. Fishtail palm. Native to Southeast Asia. Tender. Feather palms with finely divided leaves, leaflets flattened and split at tip like fish tails. Slow growing. Likes bright light, standard potting mix. Keep potting mix wet but not swimming; never let pot stand in water. Cannot prune single stem. When plants outgrow your house, move them to a sheltered outdoor patio.

C. mitus. Clustered fishtail palm. Slow grower. Light green foliage. Very tender, not for beginners.

C. ochlandra. Canton fishtail palm. Hardiest of *Caryota*. Medium dark green leaves.

C. urens. Fishtail wine palm. Dark green leaves. Dies if temperature drops below 32°.

Cast-iron plant. See Aspidistra elatior.

CATTLEYA. Large genus of epiphytic orchids native to tropical America. Most popular, best-known orchid family; includes familiar corsage orchid. Plants have pseudobulbs bearing 1-3 thick, leathery, light green leaves; 1-4 flowers per stem. Flowers in all colors except blue and black. Requires warm temperatures (60° at night, 70° or higher during the day), high humidity, good light with at least 4 hours sun daily (western or southern exposure), but protect from hot midday sun. Plant in osmunda fiber or fir bark. Water when potting mix feels dry and lightweight (about once a week). Fertilize plants with a commercial orchid fertilizer about once every 2 weeks during the growing season.

Century plant. See Agave.

CEPHALOCEREUS. Columnar cactus with white hairs; native to Mexico. Slow growing. Requires at least 4 hours of sun daily, warm temperatures. Plant in standard potting mix. Water when potting mix is completely dry.

C. palmeri. Wooly torch. Hardy. Short, blue green spines with tufts of white, wooly hair. Columnar but may branch.

C. polyanthus. Aztec column. Slow-growing column with fluted ribs, yellow brown spines.

C. senilis. Old man cactus. Ribbed column; spines hidden in long, white hairs.

C. polyanthus

CEROPEGIA woodii. Rosary vine, String of hearts. Fast-growing succulent vine native to South Africa. Hanging or trailing stems grow from a tuberous base. Heart-shaped leaves in pairs on purplish stem are dark green marbled in silver. Tiny pink or purple flowers. Small tubers that form on stems inspired the nickname "rosary vine." Plant in sandy potting mix with extra humus; water when potting mix is dry to the touch. Likes average house temperatures, filtered sunlight. Occasionally, when the plant may appear to wilt, it is only resting, so hold back on water until new growth appears. Start new plants from cuttings.

CHAMAECEREUS silvestri. Peanut cactus. Dwarf cactus native to Argentina. Cylindrical, ribbed, spiny joints that fall off easily and root just as easily. Heavy blooming in spring, summer. Bright red flowers to 3 inches long. Likes sun, warm temperatures, sandy potting mix. Let potting mix become dry between waterings.

CHAMAEDOREA. Generally slow-growing palm native to tropical America. Likes filtered light (can tolerate poor light; sun fades leaf color), average house temperatures and humidity, standard potting mix. Water occasionally; plants in good light situations will need more. See photos on pages 74 and 75.

C. elegans

C. costaricana. Bamboolike clumps grow quickly to 8-10 feet if well watered and fertilized. Lacy, leathery leaves. May need a large container.

C. elegans (Neanthe bella). Parlor palm. Best indoor *Chamaedorea*. Tolerates low light, crowded roots. Grows slowly to 3-4 feet. Fertilize regularly.

CHAMAERANTHEMUM. Foliage in different colors with veined patterns. May have small flowers. Likes standard potting mix, high humidity, filtered light, average house temperatures, evenly moist potting mix (never soggy).

C. gaudichaudii. Small creeper from Brazil. Silver-dark green leaves.

C. igneum. Suedelike leaves veined red, yellow.

C. gaudichaudii

CHAMAEROPS humilis. Mediterranean fan palm. Indoor-outdoor plant. Hardy palm rarely exceeds 4-6 feet indoors. Leaves green to bluish green, very spiny; keep out of traffic pattern. Likes at least 4 hours sun daily, standard potting mix, average house temperatures. Water heavily in summer to encourage growth. Fertilize in spring, summer.

Chenille plant. See Acalypha hispida.

Chinese evergreen. See Aglaonema.

Chinese lantern. See Abutilon.

CHLOROPHYTUM comosum. Spider plant. Evergreen plant native to tropics. Clumps of curving leaves like long, broad grass blades. Foliage green, or green variegated with white or yellow as margins or center strips. Tiny white flowers. Miniature duplicates of the mother plant, complete with roots, form at end of long, curved stem. Plantlets can be potted individually. Great display in hanging basket. Likes bright light, standard potting mix, average house temperatures and humidity. Let potting mix dry out between waterings. See photo on page 47.

Chocolate soldier. See Episcia cupreata.

Christmas cactus. See Schlumbergera bridgesii.

CHRYSALIDO-CARPUS lutescens (*Areca lutescens*). Slow-growing palm native to Malagasy. Can be summered outdoors on shaded patio. Smooth trunks, yellowish green leaves. Likes bright light, warm temperatures, standard potting mix. Water well during growing season; never let pot sit in water. Fertilize regularly in spring and summer. Spider mite can be a problem. Tricky to maintain.

CIBOTIUM glaucum (*C. chamissoi*). Hawaiian tree fern. Indoor-outdoor plant. Tree fern with feathery, golden green fronds. Likes indirect light, warm temperatures, high humidity. Plant in ½ standard potting mix, ½ peat moss or leaf mold. Keep potting mix moist but not too wet. Can spread; has very broad leaf crowns.

(Continued on page 36)

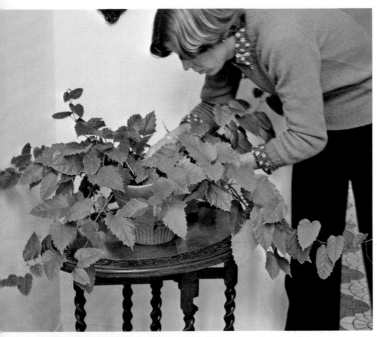

Cissus antarctica. *See page 36.*

Dracaena fragrans 'Massangeana'. *See page 41.*

Aglaonema commutatum. *See page 28.*

Dieffenbachia picta.
See page 41.

Tolmiea menziesii. *See page 76.*

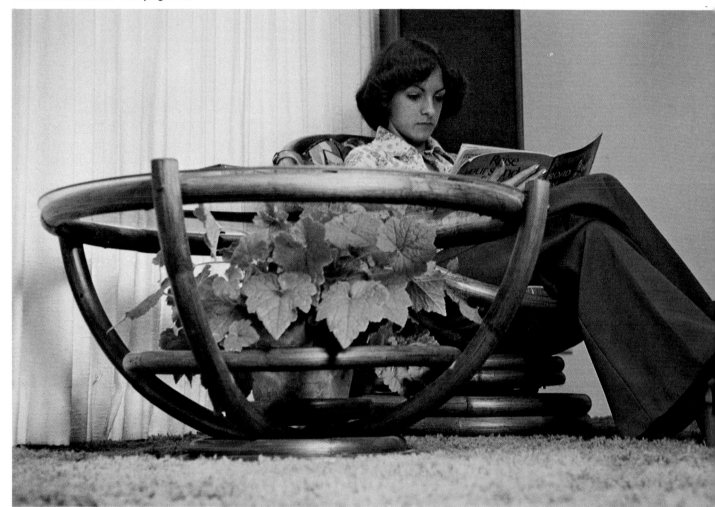

Easy plants for the beginner

If you are new to the house plant game, the plants pictured on these two pages can help make your first gardening experience a positive one. These plants adapt easily to the environment found inside most homes. Even with less than perfect light situations, low levels of humidity, and inconsistent amounts of water and fertilizer, these plants will survive. With proper treatment, they will thrive!

Most indoor gardeners learn from the mistakes made on their first house plants. But if your initial efforts involve these forgiving plants, the errors need not be fatal ones. And once you've gained your indoor gardening confidence, you can move on to more demanding house plants.

CISSUS. Evergreen vines. All climb by tendrils. Related to Virginia creeper, Boston ivy, and grape. Easy to grow. Likes average light, temperatures, humidity; standard potting mix. Water when soil dries out. Tolerant of adverse conditions. Start new plants from stem cuttings.

C. rhombifolia

C. antarctica. Kangaroo treebine. Native to Australia. Medium green, shiny, toothed leaves to 2-3½ inches long. See photo on page 34.

C. a. 'Minima'. Dwarf kangaroo ivy. Waxy green leaves on compact plant.

C. discolor. Moss green, quilted leaves with red veins, silver markings. To 6 inches long. Toothed margin. More difficult to maintain than other *Cissus.*

C. rhombifolia. Grape ivy. Native to South America. Dark green leaves in threes, sharp-toothed edges. Has bronze tones because of reddish hairs on veins underneath. Tolerates low light.

C. striata. Miniature grape ivy.

CLERODENDRUM thomsoniae. Bleeding heart, Glorybower. Large evergreen vine native to west Africa. Oval, dark green, ribbed leaves. Flowers: white, lanternlike calyx opens to show red petals. Can be trained upright on supports or as a hanger. Prune to keep compact and for more blooms. Likes warm temperatures, bright

light, some humidity, standard potting mix. Fertilize regularly during spring, summer. Keep potting mix constantly moist during growing season; less water needed in winter. See photo on page 58.

CLIVIA miniata. Kaffir lily. Evergreen perennial with tuberous roots native to South Africa. Dark green, bladelike leaves 1½ feet long. Brilliant clusters of orange, funnel-shaped flowers. Blooms from December to April. Plant in rich soil. Likes bright light (no direct sun), potting mix watered when dry to touch during active growth. Fertilize 2 or 3 times during growing season. Repot carefully every 2-3

years; *Clivia* likes crowded roots. Divide when new plants form at base. See photo on page 59.

CODIAEUM. Croton. Tropical plant grown for colorful, leathery, glossy leaves that may be green, yellow, red, purple, bronze, pink, or almost any combination of these. Many leaf shapes. Plant grows to 15 inches (can grow much taller in ideal conditions). Likes bright light, warm temperatures, high humidity, standard potting mix, lots of water.

C. aucubaefolium

Mist frequently to clean leaves, discourage pests. Large plants can be air layered. See photo on page 51.

C. aucubaefolium. Gold dust plant. Bushy plant with bright green, glossy, spotted or blotched yellow leaves.

C. spirale. Multicolored, corkscrew-twisted leaves in reds, dark gray green.

C. variegatum. Glossy, lance-shaped leaves in spectacular shades of green, yellow, red, purple, bronze.

COELOGYNE. Epiphytic evergreen orchid native to eastern hemisphere. Dark green, spoon-shaped leaves. Small flowers in shades of brown, cream, beige, or green. Likes shade or filtered light, 55°-60° nighttime temperatures, regular fertilizing during growing season. Plant in osmunda fiber or fir bark. Excess water in new growth where flower cluster forms may cause buds to rot.

COFFEA arabica. Coffee tree. Glossy, dark green, oval leaves. Small, fragrant white flowers followed by red berries; each berry contains two coffee beans. Likes filtered light, standard potting mix, average temperatures, high humidity. Keep potting mix moist but not soggy. Fertilize during growing season. Pinch to keep compact. See photo on page 42.

COLEUS blumei. Coleus. Painted nettle. Brilliantly colored, velvety leaves, often ruffled or scalloped, in shades of green, chartreuse, yellow, salmon, peach, orange, red, magenta, purple, and brown. Leaves may contain one or several colors. Needs balanced light (too much sun or too much shade causes leaf colors to fade), warm temperatures, standard

potting mix, regular fertilizing, ample water. Frequent pinching needed to encourage branching, control size.

Remove flower buds. Grow new plants from cuttings. See photo on page 51.

COLOCASIA esculenta *(Caladium esculentum).* Taro, Elephant's ear. Large perennial with tuberous roots. Native to tropical Asia and Polynesia. Mammoth, heart-shaped, gray green leaves give exotic effect. Can be summered outdoors on shaded patio. Plant tubers in rich, moist soil. Needs warm temperatures, filtered light. Keep potting mix constantly moist and fertilize monthly during growing season.

COLUMNEA. Many species native to tropical America. Trailing stems good in hanging baskets. Many leaf shapes, either glossy or hairy. Brilliantly colored, tubular flowers to 3 inches long in red, orange, yellow, or combinations of these. Plant in packaged African violet potting mix to which small pebbles, sand, or perlite has been added. Likes average house temperatures (slightly cooler than African violets), high humidity, good light. Keep potting mix moist but not soggy. Fertilize regularly during growing season. To propagate, use stem cuttings.

C. microphylla. Tiny coppery leaves.

Coral aloe. See Aloe striata.

Coral beads. See Sedum stahlii.

CORDYLINE *(Dracaena).* Evergreen, palmlike shrubs. Long, bladelike leaves. Likes at least 4 hours sun daily, warm temperatures, high humidity (use humidity trays), standard potting mix. Keep potting mix moist during growing season; less water needed in winter.

C. stricta. Dark green leaves with hint of purple. Lavender flowers. Cut canes to keep plant compact.

C. terminalis

C. terminalis. Ti. Plants may be started from "logs" —sections of stem imported from Hawaii. Can tolerate low light. Leaves have red or yellow color variation.

Corn plant. See Dracaena fragrans.

Crab cactus. See Schlumbergera truncata.

CRASSULA. Large family of succulents mostly native to South Africa. Thick, fleshy leaves. Don't count on flowers indoors. Plants can be summered outdoors. Likes sun, warm temperatures, potting mix consisting of ½ standard potting mix, ½ sharp sand. Will tolerate less than perfect conditions. Give water when potting mix dries out but never let plants shrink. Propagate by leaf or stem cuttings. See photo on page 78.

C. argentea

C. arborescens. Silver dollar. Branching plant similar to jade with gray green, red-edged, red-dotted leaves.

C. argentea. Jade plant. Bright green, rounded leaves diffused with red. Branching, shrubby growth. Plants will stay small in small containers. 'Sunset' leaves are yellow, green, and red.

C. cooperi. Low growing with narrow green leaves dotted red.

C. cultrata. Propeller plant. Light green succulent leaves twisted in opposite directions.

Creeping Charlie. See Pilea nummulariaefolia.

Creeping fig. See Ficus pumila.

CROSSANDRA infundibuliformis. Evergreen plant native to India. Grows to 1-1½ feet in 4-5-inch pot. Glossy, very dark green, gardenialike foliage. Showy flowers in scarlet orange or coral orange during summer; remove when spent. Likes strong filtered light, warm temperatures, high humidity, standard potting mix.

Keep potting mix constantly moist but never soggy (roots should never dry out completely). Mist frequently.

Croton. See Codiaeum.

Crown of thorns. See Euphorbia milii.

CRYPTANTHUS zonatus. Zebra plant. Bromeliad native to Brazil. Grown for showy leaves. Low-growing rosette clusters to 18 inches wide. Leaves wavy, dark brown red, banded crosswise with green,

(Continued on page 40)

Plants for dark places

Most houses have at least one spot where a plant would be just the right touch but where only a limited amount of light is available. These spots are just too dark for most plants, but there are several that can tolerate lower light levels.

The foliage plants pictured here can be easily maintained where light is at a minimum. Even these plants need some light to survive, though, and a corner or hall that is truly in the dark will have to remain plantless.

Ficus lyrata. *See page 45.*

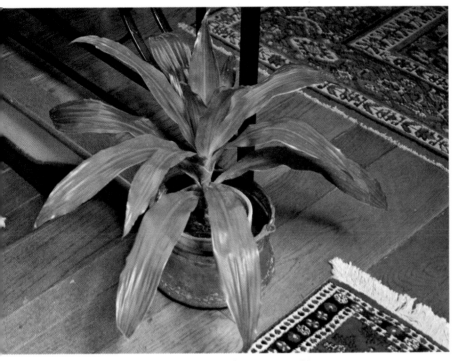

Dracaena deremensis 'Janet Craig'. *See page 41.*

Philodendron 'Majesty'. *See page 64.*

Spathiphyllum. *See page 73.*

Aspidistra elatior.
See page 29.

Philodendron oxycardium.
See page 64.

brown, or white. Likes bright light, warm temperatures. Plant in equal parts coarse sand, ground bark or peat moss, and shredded or chopped osmunda. Water thoroughly when potting mix dries out. Divide when new plant forms at base.

CTENANTHE. Related to the *Maranta*. Grown for unusual foliage; leaves may be short-stalked along the stem or long-stalked and rising from the base. Insignificant white flowers. Likes good filtered light, moist standard potting mix, warm temperatures, high humidity, regular fertilizing. Propagate from stem cuttings. See photo, page 75.

C. compressa

C. 'Burle Marx'. To 15 inches. Leaves gray green above, feathered with dark green; maroon underneath. Leaf stalks maroon.

C. compressa (Bamburanta arnoldiana). Bamburanta. Plants to 2-3 feet. Leathery oblong leaves, unequal sided to 15 inches long, waxy green on top, gray green beneath.

C. oppenheimiana. Narrow, leathery leaves, dark green banded with silver above, purple beneath.

CYCAS revoluta. Sago palm. Slow growing, usually with single trunk. In youth (2-3 feet tall), *Cycas* has airy, lacy appearance of ferns. With age (10 feet maximum height), it looks more like a palm. Actually, related to conifers. Leaves divide into narrow, leathery, dark glossy green segments. Makes offsets. Likes filtered light, standard potting mix, average house temperatures. Needs a constant supply of water but hates wet feet. Fertilize during growing season.

CYCLAMEN persicum. Florist's cyclamen. Gift plant from late fall to spring. Dark green leaves with silver markings. Flowers in pinks, reds, white resemble shooting stars. To prolong indoor bloom, give plants cool temperatures, bright light (no direct sun). Keep potting mix moist. After blooms are spent, let foliage die back; then plant tubers outdoors or discard plant. Second bloom from forced gift plant difficult.

CYMBIDIUM. Terrestrial orchid native to high altitudes in Southeast Asia. Can also be grown outdoors, brought indoors while in bloom. Long, narrow, grasslike foliage. Hybrid varieties have large flowers in white, pink, yellow, green, bronze with dark markings. Twelve or more flowers per stem. Miniature varieties have flowers about ¼ the size. Need cool nighttime temperatures (45°-55°) in summer and fall to set flower buds. Give bright light, no direct sun. Foliage should be yellow green; dark green foliage indicates that plant has had too much shade. Plant in packaged *Cymbidium* orchid potting mix or mix 2 parts each fir bark, leaf mold, and peat moss and 1 part sand. Keep potting mix constantly moist from March through October. Fertilize every 2 weeks from January through July, once a month August through December. Keep *Cymbidiums* potbound for better blooms. When dividing, keep a minimum of 3 healthy bulbs per pot. See photos on pages 59 and 66.

CYPERUS. Indoor-outdoor plant. Perennial grown for striking form. Rushlike plant related to papyrus with an umbrella-shaped cluster of leaves on top of slender stems. Likes bright light, cool temperatures, standard potting mix, high humidity. Requires constant moisture; best to submerge roots in water. Divide when clumps become too large; save smaller outside divisions and discard older center. Fertilize regularly in spring, summer.

C. alternifolius. Umbrella plant. Two to 4-foot stems. Leaves arranged like ribs of an umbrella give plant its nickname. Flowers in dry, greenish brown clusters.

C. alternifolius

C. a. 'Nanus'. Dwarf form.

C. haspan. Dwarf papyrus. Stems to 18 inches. Long, thin leaves and flowers make filmy brown and green clusters. Delicate shape.

CYRTOMIUM falcatum. Holly fern. Native to Japan. Leaflets large, dark green, leathery, glossy, toothed like Christmas holly (which plant resembles). Grows to 2-3 feet. Good indoor fern; requires less humidity than most. Likes filtered light (sunless north exposure good), average house temperatures, moist standard potting mix. When repotting, do not bury root ball.

DAVALLIA. Group of ferns with brownish, furry, creeping stems (rhizomes) that grow above ground. Stems give nicknames (see below) because they resemble animals' feet. All forms good in hanging baskets or on pedestals. Fronds feathery, dark green. Like filtered light (sunless north exposure best), cool temperatures, high humidity. Mist frequently or use humidity trays.

D. fijiensis

Plant in ½ standard potting mix, ½ peat moss. Keep potting mix moist but don't overwater. Feed occasionally. See photo on page 71.

D. fijiensis. Rabbit's foot fern. Brown, wooly, creeping rhizomes.

D. trichomanoides. Squirrel's foot fern. Large fronds to 12 inches tall. Light reddish brown rhizomes.

Devil's ivy. See Rhaphidophora aurea.

DIEFFENBACHIA. Dumb cane, Mother-in-law plant. Evergreen foliage plant native to tropical America. Nickname "dumb cane" refers to fact that the acrid sap in leaves will burn mouth and throat and may paralyze vocal cords. Usually single stem; older plants may develop multiple stems. Grows to 6 feet or taller. Large, pointed, variegated leaves; colors vary from dark green to

D. picta

yellow green and chartreuse, with variegation in white or pale cream. Likes filtered light (sunless northern exposure good), standard potting mix, average house temperatures and humidity. Water when potting mix feels dry. Fertilize regularly in spring, summer. Air layer leggy plants. See photo on page 34.

D. amoena. To 6 feet or higher. Dark green, 18-inch leaves with white stripes on either side of midrib.

D. picta. Wide, oval green leaves with greenish white dots and patches; to 10 inches long.

DIONAEA muscipula. Venus flytrap. Insect-eating plant native to the Carolinas. Does not need insects to survive. Yellow green leaves edged with hairs, hinged at center. Grows to 6 inches. Full sun brings out deep red coloring inside open leaf. Likes high humidity (especially good in terrariums), cool temperatures (around 60°), lots of water. Plant in sphagnum moss mixed with a little sand and peat moss.

DIZYGOTHECA elegantissima (*Aralia elegantissima*). Threadleaf, false aralia. Lacy, evergreen leaves that are dark green, glossy above, reddish brown underneath. Leaves divided fanwise into very narrow, 4 to 9-inch-long leaflets with notched edges. Likes bright light (no direct sun), standard potting mix with good drainage, high humidity, average house temperatures. Improper watering may cause problems; dry or waterlogged soil causes leaf drop. Fertilize regularly.

Donkey tail. See Sedum morganianum.

DRACAENA (Cordyline). Evergreen palmlike plants. Long, bladelike foliage, either green or variegated. Can become tall. Likes bright light, standard potting mix, average house temperatures and humidity, regular fertilizing and watering. Will tolerate abuse —low light, low humidity, infrequent watering. Effective when planted 3 to a pot. See photos on pages 34 and 39.

D. f. 'Massangeana'

D. deremensis 'Janet Craig'. Green, sword-shaped leaves.

D. deremensis 'Warneckii'. Leaves 2 feet long, 2 inches wide; rich green with white and gray streaks running lengthwise.

D. draco. Dragon tree. Slow growing with unusual form. Heavy, sword-shaped leaves.

D. fragrans. Corn plant. Green, cornlike leaves.

D. f. 'Massangeana'. Green, cornlike leaves with broad yellow stripe in center of leaf.

D. godseffiana. Gold dust plant. Small, slow grower. Dark green leaves irregularly spotted with yellow or white.

D. marginata. Blade-shaped, deep olive green leaves edged with red. Needs bright light to maintain color.

Dumb cane. See Dieffenbachia.

DYCKIA fosteriana. A bromeliad native to tropical America. Leaves of silvery gray, occasionally reddish brown, in rosette form with spike-toothed edges, sharp tips. Orange flowers on tall, slender stems. Likes full sun (don't let foliage burn), average house temperatures

and humidity, regular fertilizing. Plant in equal parts standard potting mix, sand, and peat moss or fir bark. Let potting mix dry out between waterings.

(Continued on page 44)

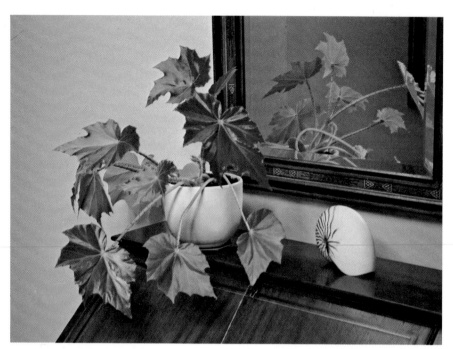

Begonia, rhizomatous. *See page 30.*

Hypocyrta nummularia. *See page 52.*

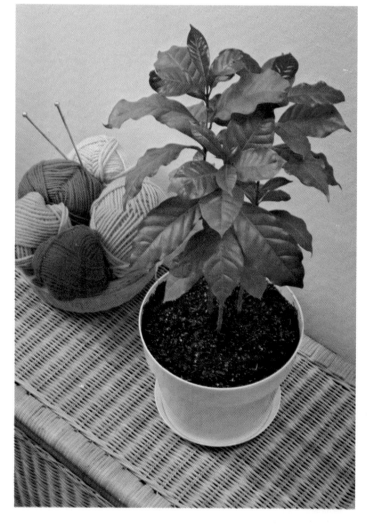

Coffea arabica.
See page 36.

From left: **Peperomia obtusifolia; P. caperata 'Emerald Ripple'; P. sandersii.** *See page 61.*

Green leaves come in many hues, shapes, sizes, and textures. The sampling shown here gives you an idea of their diversity. Since these house plants will be grown for their green foliage, you should cater to their light and fertilizing needs (to keep the green green) and give them frequent baths for shiny, dust-free leaves.

If you like plants with green foliage

Saintpaulia ionantha. *See page 68.*

Kalanchoe blossfeldiana. *See page 53.*

Beaucarnea recurvata. *See page 30.*

Schefflera arboricola. *See page 69.*

ECHEVERIA. Succulent native to the Americas. Rosette form with fleshy leaves of green or gray green, sometimes marked with deeper colors. Flowers form in clusters on long stems, are bell-shaped in pink, red, yellow. Likes full sun, warm temperatures. Plant in equal parts sharp sand, standard potting mix. Water when potting mix is completely dry to touch.

E. imbricata

E. derenbergii. Painted lady. Small, tight, spreading rosettes. Leaves grayish white with red edges. Reddish and yellow flowers.

E. elegans. Mexican snowball. Silver blue rosette frosted white. Pink flowers.

E. glauca. Hen and chicks. Purple tinted, gray green rosettes.

E. imbricata. Hen and chicks. Gray green rosettes.

E. pulvinata. Round hairy leaves covered with silvery down that later turns red. Red flowers.

ECHINOCACTUS grusonii. Golden barrel. Cactus with cylindrical shape native to Mexico. Slow growing. Straight, sharp, yellow spines; with age, develops crown of yellow wool. Yellow flowers. Likes sun, warm temperatures. Plant in equal parts standard potting mix, sharp sand. Let potting mix completely dry out between waterings; in winter, give only enough to keep plant from shrinking or shriveling.

ECHINOCEREUS. Desert cactus requiring little attention. Usually less than 12 inches tall. Ornamental spines, showy flowers. Likes warm temperatures, full sun. Plant in equal parts standard potting mix, sharp sand; occasional water.

E. baileyi. Columnar growth, white spines. Yellow flowers.

E. dasyacanthus. Rainbow cactus. Small, columnar plant covered with soft spines. Has large yellow flowers.

E. ehrenbergii. Stem erect, free-branching from base; glassy white spines. Purple red flowers.

E. baileyi

E. reichenbachii. Lace cactus. Small, heavily spined. Red and yellow flowers.

ECHINOPSIS. Easter lily cactus, Sea urchin cactus. Small cylindrical or globular cactus native to South America. Large showy flowers in white, yellow, pink, red. Free blooming in summer if given good light, frequent fertilizing. Likes at least 4 hours of sun daily, warm temperatures. Plant in equal parts standard potting mix, sharp sand. Water when soil dries.

Elephant's ear. See Colocasia esculenta.

Emerald ripple. See Peperomia caperata.

EPIDENDRUM. Easy-to-grow orchids native to tropical America, epiphytic or terrestrial. Variable in flower and plant form. Some have pseudobulbs and require a rest after flowering; others are cane-stemmed and need moisture all year. Flowers in many colors. Plant in ground fir bark, osmunda fiber, or packaged orchid potting mix. Most like sun, warm temperatures, and high humidity. Fertilize regularly.

E. atropurpureum. To 16 inches with pseudobulbs. Three-inch, chocolate brown and pale green flowers with white and purple markings; 4-20 flowers per stem. Bloom spring, early summer. Rest plants after blooming.

E. ibaguense *(E. radicans).* Native to Colombia. To 2-4 feet with reedlike, leafy stems. Dense flower clusters. Orange yellow flowers with fringed lip. Numerous hybrids with flowers in yellow, orange, pink, red, lavender, white; generally sold by color.

E. nemorale. To 16 inches. Large, 4-inch, rose and purple flowers. Blooms spring, summer.

E. stamfordianum. To 30 inches with tiny yellow and red flowers. Pseudobulb. Blooms spring.

EPIPHYLLUM. Orchid cactus. Epiphytic jungle cactus. Can be summered outdoors on shaded patio. Spineless, has flattened stems with scalloped edges. Large, showy flowers in many colors bloom April to June. Plant in sandy soil with good drainage. Keep plant potbound for best results. Likes bright light, cool nighttime temperatures (50°), high humidity. Let potting mix dry out thoroughly between waterings. Rest plants in winter. Natural growth is pendent; stake plants for upright growth.

EPISCIA. Peacock plant, Flame violet. Oval, 4-inch, velvety-hairy foliage colored from green to brown with metallic sheen in silver, bronze, green; frequently veined or mottled in contrasting colors. Leaf type similar to African violets. *Episcia* produces runners like strawberries, with plantlets forming at runner ends; growth ideal for hanging baskets. Tubular flowers usually red orange, but hybrid plant colors include pink, yellow, white, lavender, combinations. Likes warm temperatures (60° or higher at night, 75° during day), high hu-

E. cupreata

midity, bright light (no direct sun), regular fertilizing, lots of water (more than for African violets). Plant in packaged African violet potting mix. Can propagate from stem cuttings. See photo on page 51.

E. cupreata. Oval coppery leaves. Orange red flowers. Variety 'Metallica' has olive green leaves with pale stripes, red margins. 'Chocolate Soldier' has chocolate brown, silver-veined leaves.

E. reptans (E. fulgens). Pebbled bronze leaves with willow green veins. Red flowers.

EUPHORBIA. Spurge. Large group of plants, many succulents. Most have acrid, milky sap (poisonous in some species) that can irritate skin. "Flower" is really colored bracts; true flowers are centered in bracts. Give strong, filtered light; warm, even temperatures. Plant in equal parts standard potting mix, sharp sand. Watering differs among species. Fertilize during growing seasons.

E. hermentiana (E. trigona). Slow growing. Interesting silhouette. Three-angled, toothed stems with fleshy wings at each angle. Small, oblong leaves. Can tolerate drought but prefers regular watering.

E. lactea 'Cristata'. Dwarf, crested, bizarre form resembles E. hermentiana with same water needs. Broad, green and gray, coralloid mass to 12 inches.

E. hermentiana

E. milii. Crown of thorns. Succulent, woody perennial native to Malagasy. Legend says flowers were once white but turned red when stems were used to make the crown of thorns Jesus wore. Tall stems to 3-4 feet; long, sharp thorns. Leaves roundish, thin, light green, found only near branch ends. Red bracts (yellow, orange, pink varieties also). Needs bright light, no direct sun. May bloom all year. Can tolerate drought but prefers regular watering.

E. obesa. Baseball plant. Succulent. Fleshy, gray green cylinder to 8 inches tall with brownish striplings, brown dots that resemble stitching on a baseball. Keep dryish in winter.

E. 'Pink Sensation'. Hummel hybrid, known as giant crown of thorns or Christ thorn hybrids. Larger stems, leaves, and flowers than E. milii. Blooms continuously. Likes regular watering.

E. pulcherrima. Poinsettia. Usually a blooming Christmas gift plant. Bracts in red (most common), pink, white. To prolong bloom, keep in sunny window with constant temperatures. Keep potting mix moist. After blooming, cut stems back to 2 buds, reduce water, keep in cool spot, and then set outside (when all danger of frost is past) in sun. Difficult to repeat blooming indoors.

FATSHEDERA lizei. Vine that climbs like ivy. Hybrid between *Fatsia japonica* and *Hedera helix*. Highly polished leaves with 3-5 pointed lobes, 6-8 inches wide. Likes bright light (protect from hot sun), average house temperatures and humidity, standard potting mix, ample water. Prune to keep compact. Needs support to climb. Use stem cuttings to propagate.

F. l. 'Variegata'. White-bordered leaves.

FATSIA japonica *(Aralia sieboldii, A. japonica).* Japanese aralia. Tropical evergreen shrub with glossy, dark green, deeply lobed, fanlike leaves. Small, whitish flowers fall, winter; remove flower buds for better foliage. Use young plants indoors; prune or pinch to keep compact. Likes bright light, cool temperatures (not over 70°), standard potting mix, regular waterings.

F. j. 'Moseri'. Compact, low growing.

F. j. 'Variegata'. Leaves edged golden yellow to creamy white.

FERN. Large group of perennial plants grown for foliage. Leaves are usually finely cut. No flowers. They reproduce by spores that form directly on the fronds. Though most are native to forests, some grow in deserts, in open fields, or near timberline in high mountains. Tree ferns may grow to 50 feet or more. Native ferns are smaller, with handsome fronds. Most like rich potting mix, filtered light, and lots of moisture. All ferns look best if groomed; remove dead or injured fronds by cutting off near the soil surface. Fertilize during growing season. For ferns that will grow indoors, see *Asplenium, Cibotium glaucum, Cyrtomium falcatum, Davallia, Humata tyermannii, Nephrolepis, Platycerium, Polystichum, Pteris.*

FICUS. Ornamental fig. Diverse family of trees, shrubs, vines. Ornamental foliage. Likes standard potting mix, bright light (no direct sun), regular fertilizing. Let soil dry out between waterings. See photos on pages 38, 62, 63, and back cover.

F. benjamina. Weeping Chinese banyan, Weeping fig. Evergreen. Shiny green leathery leaves, 2-5 inches long. New growth pale green, older leaves dark green. Drooping branches, delicate appearance.

F. diversifolia. Mistletoe fig. Evergreen. Native to Malaysia. Slow growing. Open, twisted branch pattern. Two-inch leaves are round, thick, dark green with tan specks on upper surface, black specks below. Small yellow fruits. Needs more water than other *Ficus.*

F. lyrata

F. elastica. Rubber plant. Native to India, Malaysia. Very easy house plant. Leaves thick, glossy, leathery, dark green, 8-12 inches long by 4-6 inches wide. Can tolerate drought.

F. e. 'Decora' *(F. e. 'Belgica').* Broader, glossier leaves than *F. elastica,* bronze when young.

F. e. 'Rubra'. New leaves reddish; red edge maintained as rest of leaf turns green.

F. e. 'Variegata' *(F. doescheri).* Long, narrow leaves are variegated yellow and green.

(Continued on page 48)

**Fittonia verschaffeltii
'Argyroneura'.**
See page 48.

If you like variegated foliage

Variegated foliage has stripes, veins, splotches, or spots—usually in white, yellow, or pale green—that contrast with the rest of the leaf. House plants that possess this eye-catching foliage can create points of interest in your interior landscaping scheme. They also add variety to plant groupings.

These plants may be more demanding in their growing needs than plants with green foliage; many variegated plants require higher levels of light over a longer period of time. If grown in less than adequate light they may lose some of the variegation that first attracted you.

Plectranthus oertendahlii.
See page 65.

Calathea. *See page 31.*

Tolmiea menziesii variegata. *See page 76.*

Pilea cadierei. *See page 64.*

Chlorophytum comosum. *See page 33.*

F. lyrata *(F. pandurata)*. Fiddleleaf fig. Native to tropical Africa. Large, dark green, glossy leaves, fiddle-shaped to 15 inches long, 10 inches wide. Prune top to make plant bushy. Tolerates low light. Doesn't require a large pot. Keep leaves clean.

F. pumila *(F. repens)*. Creeping fig. Evergreen vine native to China, Japan, Australia. Tiny, heart-shaped, delicate leaves. Difficult to grow indoors.

F. retusa nitida. Similar to *F. benjamina* but with straighter branches and fewer leaves. Needs frequent pruning for shape.

Fiddleleaf fig. See Ficus lyrata.

Fig, weeping. See Ficus.

Fingernail plant. See Neoregelia spectabilis.

FITTONIA verschaffeltii.

Nerve plant, Mosaic plant. Evergreen creeper native to South America. Dark green, oval leaves veined with red or bright pink. Likes indirect light (north exposure good), high humidity, warm temperatures, regular fertilizing, standard potting mix, lots of water (never let potting mix dry out completely). See photo on page 46.

F. v. 'Argyroneura'. Leaves veined white.

Flame violet. See Episcia.

Fluffy ruffles. See Nephrolepis exaltata 'Fluffy Ruffles'.

Freckle face. See Hypoestes sanguinolenta.

FUCHSIA. Lady's

eardrop. Indoor-outdoor plant. Upright or trailing stems. Trailing varieties good in hanging baskets. Bring indoors to enjoy bloom or to protect from winter frost. Beautiful flowers in many color combinations and sizes. Likes filtered light (or a shaded patio), cool temperatures, frequent fertilizing, standard potting mix with excellent drainage, high humidity. Keep potting mix constantly moist. Water daily. Propagate by stem cuttings.

GARDENIA jasminoides.
Indoor-outdoor plant. Evergreen shrub native to China. Shiny, bright green leaves. White, very fragrant flowers. Needs warm days with bright light, cool nighttime temperatures, regular fertilizing, lots of water (more than most indoor plants). Plant in equal parts standard potting mix and peat moss or ground bark. Keep potting mix constantly moist.

GASTERIA. Oxtongue. Succulent native to South America. Long, flat leaves. Likes full sun (tolerates less), average house temperatures. Plant in equal parts standard potting mix and sharp sand. Water when potting mix is completely dry to touch.

G. liliputana. Mottled dark green, pale green leaves arranged spirally.

G. verrucosa. Tapered pink, purple leaves with white, wartlike lumps.

GEOGENANTHUS undatus. Seersucker plant. Tropical plant native to Peru. Silvery green striped leaves with rich purple underneath; "seersucker" texture. Grows to 1 foot; prune to keep compact. Likes warm temperatures, filtered light, high humidity, standard potting mix. Keep potting mix moist.

Geranium. See Pelargonium.

Glorybower. See Clerodendrum thomsoniae.

Gloxinia. See Sinningia speciosa.

Gold dust plant. See Codiaeum aucubaefolium, Dracaena godseffiana.

Goldfish plant. See Hypocyrta nummularia.

Grape ivy. See Cissus rhombifolia.

GUZMANIA lingulata. Bromeliad native to tropical America. Rosette of smooth, metallic green leaves centered with red bracts; inner bracts are orange red, tipped white or yellow. Inconspicuous white flowers. Likes diffused light (direct sun may burn leaves), warm temperatures, high humidity, regular fertilizing. Plant in fast-draining, moisture-retentive potting mix. Give ample moisture and keep "vase" filled with water. Divide when new plant forms near base.

GYMNOCALYCIUM. Chin cactus. Cactus with globular bodies, regularly arranged protrusions that give nickname. Flowers are red, pink, white. Likes sun, average indoor temperatures. Plant in equal parts standard potting mix and sharp sand. Water when potting mix dries out; during winter rest give only enough water to keep plant from shriveling.

G. mihanovichii. Gray green globe. Blooms at early age.

GYNURA aurantiaca. Velvet plant. Tropical plant native to East Indies. Dark green, lance-shaped, toothed leaves covered with purple hairs give foliage a velvety appearance. Needs strong light for best leaf color, standard potting mix, average temperatures, regular fertilizing. Likes lots of water; mist foliage frequently for humidity. Flowers

have unpleasant smell; snap off all buds. Prune to keep compact. Use stem cuttings to propagate.

HAEMARIA discolor. Jewel orchid. Orchid grown for foliage instead of flowers. Striking dark green, velvety foliage with red pinstriping. Needs bright light, warm temperatures, rich potting mix with good drainage, high humidity (good in large terrariums). Don't disturb roots; plant has rhizomatic growth. Plant in large, shallow container. Fertilize during growing season.

Hare's foot fern. See Polypodium aureum.

HAWORTHIA. Succulents of the lily family native to South Africa. Variable in growth habit. Best-known ones resemble small aloes; others make small towers of neatly stacked fleshy leaves. Likes shade or sunless north exposure, average temperatures. Plant in equal parts standard potting mix and sharp sand. Let potting mix dry out between waterings.

H. fasciata. Zebra haworthia. Zebra-striped rosette. Leaves dark green; raised white dots.

H. fasciata

H. setata. Lace haworthia. Small rosette with many leaves. Dark green leaves marked with white translucent areas edged with bristly white teeth.

HEDERA helix. English ivy. Evergreen vine. Dark, dull green leaves with paler vines. Many types of growth habits. Needs constant temperatures (very little fluctuation), standard potting mix. Tolerant of low light situations. Let potting mix dry out

slightly between waterings. Soil should feel slightly damp and spongy. Fertilize every 2 months. Mist frequently to discourage mites. Prune to keep desired size and shape. A sampling of varieties follows. Propagate from stem cuttings.

H. h. 'Baltica'. Small dark green leaves with 5 deeply cut lobes.

H. h. 'Glacier'. Variegated form. Triangular, leathery, dark green leaves bordered with white. Needs more light than other varieties.

H. h. 'Hibernica'. Irish ivy. Largest of the varieties. Dense growth. Five-inch, round, deep green leaves with lighter green veining.

H. h. 'Needlepoint'. Sharply pointed, dark green leaves.

H. h. 'Sweetheart'. Heart-shaped, dark green leaves with no visible lobes.

HEIMERLIODENDRON brunonianum 'Variegatum'. Pisonia. A native of New Zealand. Grows slowly to 4 to 6 feet indoors. Variegated leaves with markings in varying shades of green with ivory border. Likes warm temperatures, standard potting mix, some sun to retain mottling. Feed and water regularly. See photo on back cover.

HEMIGRAPHIS 'Exotica'. Waffle plant, Purple waffle plant. Creeping plant with oblong, randomly puckered, metallic purplish green foliage that is dark red underneath. Likes filtered light, average room conditions, some humidity, standard potting mix kept constantly moist. Good in hanging baskets.

Hen and chicks. See Echeveria glauca, E. imbricata.

HIBISCUS rosa-sinensis. Chinese hibiscus. Tropical hibiscus. Indoor-outdoor plant. Evergreen shrub with glossy foliage; varies in size and texture. Compact varieties best in containers. Flowers 4-8 inches wide, single or double, in white, pink, red, yellow, orange, apricot. Bring indoors when frost threatens during late fall through spring. Will bloom indoors if temperatures constant at 60°-70°. Retains foliage to 40°. Likes sun, standard potting mix with excellent drainage, reg-

(Continued on page 52)

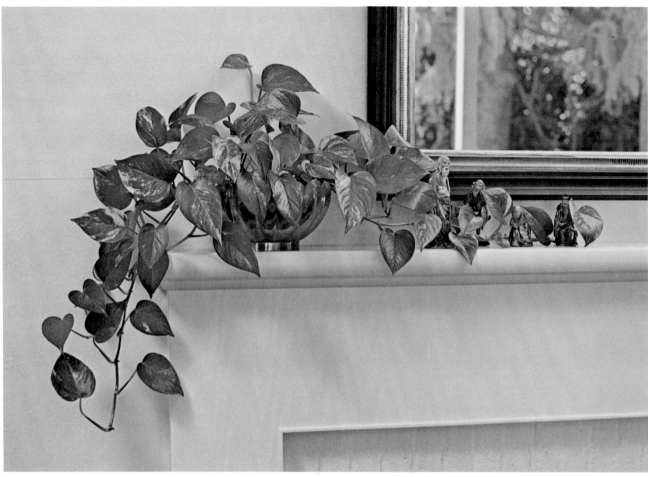

Rhaphidophora aurea. *See page 68.*

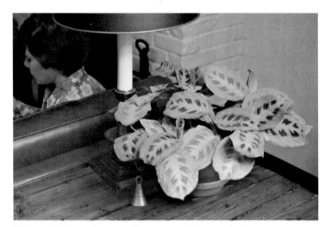

Maranta leuconeura. *See page 56.*

Abutilon striatum thompsonii. *See page 26.*

colorful foliage

Whether you choose plants with colorful foliage to suit the color scheme of a particular room or simply add a splash of brightness to liven up a dull corner, you can find house plant foliage in flamboyant pinks, reds, oranges, yellows, or purples—or, if you prefer, in subtle grays or greenish browns. The color appears as spots, veins, edges, splotches, or stripes on the leaves.

A few of these colorful plants, such as the marantas, coleus, and pothos, can be easily grown when adequate light is provided. Other plants with vivid leaves require careful attention to their growing needs. The light factor can be crucial; if these plants don't receive enough light, the colors may fade or the leaves themselves may die or fall off.

Episcia cupreata. *See page 44-45.*

Coleus blumei.
See page 36.

Maranta leuconeura 'Erythroneura'. *See page 56.*

Codiaeum variegatum.
See page 36.

ular fertilizing twice a month. Water frequently. Pruning needed to keep compact. Prune tops and, if needed, roots in fall when plant moves indoors. Return to partially shaded patio when frost danger gone, late April, May. Some compact varieties: 'Bride', 'California Gold', 'Flamingo Plume', 'Florida Sunset', 'Red Dragon', 'White Wings Compacta'.

Holly fern. See Cyrtomium falcatum.

Houseleek. See Sempervivum.

HOWEIA. Kentia palm native to Lord Howe Island in South Pacific. Slow growing. Feathery leaves drop to expose clean, green trunk ringed with leaf scars. Likes warm temperatures, standard potting mix, ample moisture. Fertilize during growing season. Tolerant of low light, some watering neglect.

H. belmoreana

H. belmoreana. Sentry palm. Arching leaves. More compact than *H. forsteriana*.

H. forsteriana. Paradise palm. Leaves to 9 feet (less indoors) with long, drooping leaflets.

HOYA. Wax flower, Wax plant. Shrubby or climbing house plant. May need support to climb. Thick, waxy leaves. Tight clusters of small, waxy flowers. Likes sun, some humidity, constant temperatures around 70°, standard potting mix. Let soil go

H. carnosa

partially dry between waterings. Plant goes semidormant in winter, requiring less light, less water (let potting mix go almost completely dry), lower temperatures. Keep plants potbound for best bloom. Fertilize every 2 months during growing season. Do not prune out flowering wood; new blossom clusters appear from stumps of old ones. To propagate, use stem cuttings.

H. bella. Shrubby. Older branches droop; good for hanging baskets. Small leaves. Tight clusters of white, purple-centered, summer flowers.

H. carnosa. Long, oval leaves. Immature leaves are red. Big, round, tight clusters of creamy white flowers; each flower has 5-pointed pink star in center. Summer blooming, fragrant.

H. c. 'Compacta'. Crinkly, closely spaced leaves.

H. c. 'Variegata'. Leaves edged in white, pink.

HUMATA tyermannii. Bear's foot fern. Small fern native to China. Furry creeping rhizomes resemble bear's feet. Fronds 8-10 inches long, very finely cut. Like *Davallia* in appearance but slower growing. Likes filtered light (sunless north exposure good), cool indoor temperatures, high humidity. Plant in equal parts standard potting mix and peat moss. Likes lots of water.

HYPOCYRTA nummularia. Goldfish plant. Pairs of shiny, thick, dark green, succulent leaves on arching branches. Good in hanging baskets. Inch-long, fat, orange flowers with pinched mouths; blooms resemble goldfish. Likes warm temperatures, high humidity, bright light (can take some morning sun), regular fertilizing. Plant in packaged African violet potting mix; give enough water at room temperature to keep mix moist. See photo on page 42.

HYPOESTES sanguinolenta. Freckle face, Pink polka dot plant. Foliage plant native to Malagasy. Long, oval, medium green leaves irregularly spotted with pink. Variety 'Splash' has larger spots. Likes filtered light, warm temperatures, some humidity, regular fertilizing. Plant in equal parts standard potting mix and peat moss; keep moisture level constant. Pinch tips to keep bushy. Use stem cuttings from new growth to propagate.

IRESINE herbstii. Blood-leaf. Foliage plant native to Brazil. Translucent, crimson or yellowish, oval leaves. Color may vary. Likes bright light (needed for best leaf color), average house temperatures and humidity, standard potting mix. Let potting mix dry out between waterings. Fertilize regularly. Needs pruning to stay compact. Root stem cuttings in water.

Iron cross begonia. See Begonia masoniana.

Ivy, English. See Hedera.

Ivy, German. See Senecio.

Ivy, grape. See Cissus.

Jade plant. See Crassula argentea.

KALANCHOE. Succulents native to Malagasy. Shapes and sizes vary. Flowers fairly large, bell-shaped. Likes sun or bright light, warm temperatures. Plant in equal parts standard potting mix and sharp sand. Water when potting mix dries out. After blooming, prune tops and hold watering until new growth starts. See photo page 59.

K. blossfeldiana

K. beharensis *(Kitchingia mandrakensis).* Felt plant. Larger than most *Kalanchoes.* Leaves at stem tips; each leaf 4-8 inches long, half as wide, triangular to lance-shaped, thick, and heavily covered with dense white to brown feltlike hairs. Foliage waved and crimped at edges. Hybrids differ in leaf size, color, degree of felting.

K. blossfeldiana. Popular Christmas gift plant. Fleshy, shiny leaves, dark green edged with red, either smooth-edged or scalloped. Small, bright red flowers in clusters. Other varieties in yellow, orange, salmon. Blooms winter, spring.

K. daigremontiana. Maternity plant. Single-stemmed. Fleshy leaves 6-8 inches long, 1¼ or more inches wide, gray green spotted in red. Leaf edges notched; new plantlets sprout in notches, giving nickname. Small, grayish purple flower clusters.

K. pinnata *(Bryophyllum pinnatum).* Air plant. Fleshy leaves; immature ones scalloped, older ones divided into 3-5 leaflets, also scalloped. Produces plantlets at the notches of the scallops. Flowers greenish white to reddish. Tolerant of low light. Likes moisture.

K. tomentosa. Panda plant. Leaves very fleshy, 2 inches long, coated with dense white hairs. Leaf tips and notches in leaves marked dark brown.

Kangaroo ivy, dwarf. See Cissus antarctica 'Minima'.

KOHLERIA. Native to tropical America. Can be staked for upright growth or allowed to hang. Rhizomatic. Fuzzy, plain green or patterned leaves. Velvety-hairy tubular flowers with flat, 5-lobed faces in reds, pinks, whites. Some have purple dots contrasting with flower color. Likes average house temperatures, filtered light, high humidity, regular fertilizing. Plant in packaged African violet potting mix kept constantly moist. Remove all old growth for continued bloom and plant health.

K. eriantha

K. amabilis. Good in hanging baskets. Leaves soft green patterned with purplish green. Flowers bright pink with darker streaks.

K. bogotensis. Dark green foliage marked in pale green or white; brownish red underneath. Flowers bright red, yellow dots.

K. eriantha. Red leaf margins. Flowers orange red with yellow markings on lower 3 lobes.

K. lindeniana. Leaves veined silver with bronze margins. Compact growth. Flowers white with violet markings.

Lady palm. See Rhapis.

Lady's slipper. See Paphiopedilum.

LAELIA. Epiphytic orchid mostly native to Mexico. *Cattleya*-type foliage and flowers. One or 2 evergreen bladelike leaves atop pseudobulbs. Flowers smaller than *Cattleyas* with narrower petals. Needs at least 4 hours sun (south or west exposure; sun needed for best flowering), warm temperatures (60° at night, at least 70° during the day), high humidity. Plant in osmunda fiber or fir bark. Let potting mix dry out between waterings. After flowering

and until new growth starts, *Laelias* need very little water. Feed plants about every 2 weeks with an orchid fertilizer during growing season.

Lily-of-the-Nile. See Agapanthus.

Lipstick plant. See Aeschynanthus lobbianus.

LITHOPS. Stoneface. Large succulent family native to South Africa. Shaped like an inverted cone; top resembles a stone with a fissure across the middle. From this fissure emerge a large flower (looks like an ice plant flower) and new leaves. Likes sun, warm temperatures. Plant in equal

parts standard potting mix and sharp sand. Water when potting mix is dry to touch in summer; needs no water during winter.

LIVISTONA chinensis. Chinese fountain palm. Palm native from China to Australia. Slow growing. Best in large areas. Roundish, bright green, shiny leaves droop at outer edge. Leaf-scarred trunk; old leaves are self-pruning. Likes bright

(Continued on page 56)

Some house plants—those that grow in a drooping or spreading habit—can best be shown off by suspension. By dangling them from a ceiling hook or wall bracket or letting them spill over a high perch, you display them to their best advantage.

Caring for a pendent plant can be troublesome. Hanging plants tend to dry out rapidly, requiring frequent watering. And their overhead position makes watering more difficult. You will need to provide a waterproof drip saucer to prevent furniture damage, or take plants to a sink or tub for watering. Also, choose their location carefully; a suspended plant can become a formidable obstacle.

Plants that take to the air

Syngonium podophyllum. *See page 76.*

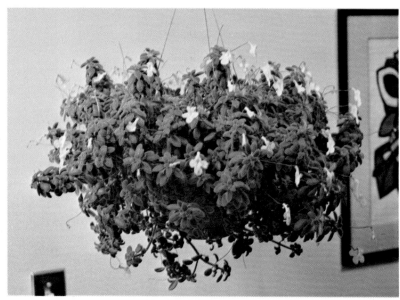

Streptocarpus saxorum.
See page 76.

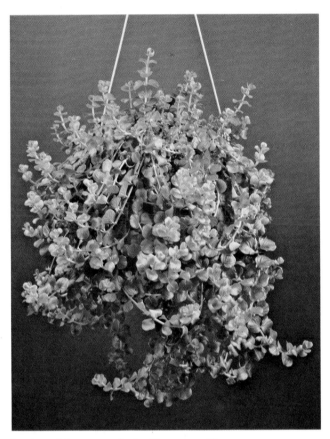

Lysimachia nummularia. *See page 56.*

Tradescantia multiflora. *See page 76.*

Asparagus densiflorus 'Sprengeri'. *See page 29.*

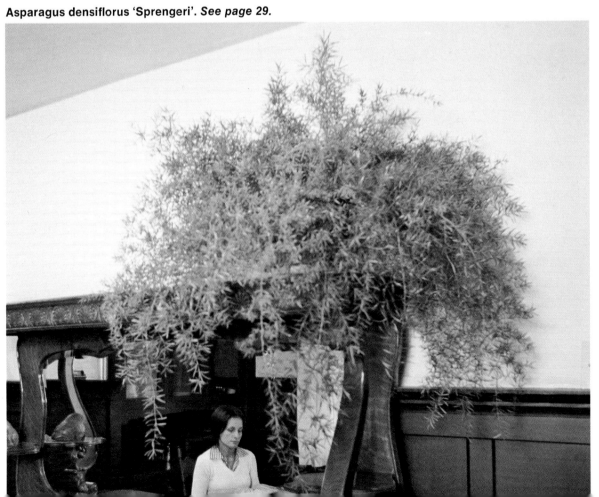

light, average temperatures, standard potting mix, ample water. Fertilize during growing season.

LOBIVIA. Small globular or cylindrical-shaped cactus. Large showy flowers in red, yellow, pink, orange, purplish lilac. Many available species. Likes sun, warm temperatures. Plant in equal parts standard potting mix and sharp sand. Water when potting mix is almost dry to touch during growing season, less in winter. Fertilize only during growing season. See photo on page 79.

    L. ferox. Plant has large, sturdy spines.

LYCASTE. Epiphytic and terrestrial orchids native to Central America. Large pseudobulbs bear 1-3 plaited leaves. Long - lasting, predominantly green flowers; some in pink, white, yellow, brown. Likes cool temperatures (50°-65°), bright light (no direct sun), high humidity. Plant in fibrous loam with enough sphagnum moss and leaf mold to be well drained. Keep potting mix

L. deppei

moist except for the period after flowering, when watering should be minimal until new growth appears.

    L. aromatica. To 16 inches. Bright yellow, fragrant flowers in winter.

    L. deppei. To 28 inches. Greenish white flowers dotted brown. Blooms at various times during year.

    L. skinneri. To 30 inches. White or pink flowers spotted rose to red in winter.

LYSIMACHIA nummularia. Moneywort, Creeping Jennie. Evergreen creeping plant with long runners. Can be summered outdoors on shaded patio. Good in hanging baskets. Light green, roundish leaves. Yellow flowers form singly at leaf joints in summer. Needs bright light (no direct sun), standard potting mix, average temperatures, some humidity, ample water. Keep compact. See photo on page 55.

Maidenhair fern. See Adiantum.

MAMMILLARIA. Small, cylindrical or globe-shaped cactus either single-stemmed or clustered. Small flowers in red, pink, yellow, white. Likes sun, warm temperatures. Plant in equal parts standard potting mix and sharp sand. Give ample water in summer, less during winter. Many species available. See photo on page 78.

    M. bocasana. Powder puff cactus. Clustered. Globe - shaped with white hairs. Yellow flowers.

    M. hahniana. Old lady cactus. Globular, spiny with long white hairs.

MARANTA leuconeura. Prayer plant. Rabbit tracks. Foliage plant native to tropical America. Low, bushy growth. Large green leaves with paired brown spots along midrib; spots turn dark green with age. At night, leaves fold together, resembling praying hands (actually the leaves are conserving moisture). Likes filtered light (leaves folding at night and opening again during the day indicate that light

MARANTA leuconeura

is sufficient), high humidity, standard potting mix, regular fertilizing, warm temperatures (above 65°), lots of water. Prune out old or straggly leaves regularly. Use stem cuttings for new plants. See photos on pages 50 and 51.

    M. l. 'Erythroneura'. Red-veined prayer plant. Olive green leaves with jagged silver center and red veins.

    M. l. 'Kerchoveana'. Undersurface of leaves gray spotted with red.

    M. l. 'Massangeana'. Large leaves with prominent veins and pink spots, purple underneath.

Martha Washington geranium. See Pelargonium.

Maternity plant. See Kalanchoe diagremontiana.

Mexican snowball. See Echeveria elegans.

MILTONIA. Pansy orchid. Epiphytic orchid native to tropical, subtropical Americas. Long, graceful, light green, bladelike leaves produce a clump of foliage, 10-12 inches tall and wide, above short pseudobulbs. Flowers, single or in clusters, are flat, velvety, resemble pansies; whites, yellows, reds, or blends of these colors are sometimes spotted or patterned. Likes filtered light (no direct sun; can tolerate low light, but dark green foliage

indicates too little light), average house temperatures (70°-80°), humidity. Plant in osmunda fiber or ground fir bark. Keep potting mix constantly moist when flower spikes form; water less frequently in winter. Feed weekly with half-strength fertilizer.

MIMOSA pudica. Sensitive plant. Tender perennial native to Guatemala. Feathery, grass green leaves fold temporarily when touched, quickly recover. Likes bright light (some sun), warm house temperatures, high humidity, standard potting mix kept moist (avoid overwatering). Good for demonstrating plant movement; children find them fascinating.

Ming aralia. See Polyscias fruticosa 'Elegans'.

Ming fern. See Asparagus retrofractus.

Mistletoe fig. See Ficus diversifolia.

MONSTERA deliciosa
(Philodendron pertusum).
Split-leaf philodendron.
Large vining plant native to
tropical America. Requires
good support to climb.
Leathery, dark green
leaves, deeply cut and per-
forated with holes. Long,
cordlike roots hanging from
stems will root if pushed
into the soil; may be re-
moved if preferred. Callalike flowers may form on
mature plant. If heat, light,
and humidity are high, the
flower spike may ripen into

edible fruit. Likes bright light (can tolerate from part-
time sun to sunless light), standard potting mix, warm
temperatures, high humidity, ample water. Feed occasionally. Wipe or wash leaves frequently to clean.
Smaller leaves or leaves that fail to split indicate poor
light, low humidity. Propagate by air layering.

Mosaic plant. See Fittonia verschaffeltii.

**Moses-in-the-cradle, Moses-in-the-boat. See Rhoeo
spathacea.**

Mother fern. See Asplenium bulbiferum.

Mother-in-law plant. See Dieffenbachia.

Moth orchid. See Phalaenopsis.

MUSA. Bana-
na. Tender pe-
rennial tree
may form
clumps. Dwarf
forms (2-5 feet
tall) best in-
doors. May be
summered out-
doors; protect
from wind.
Large, broad,
shiny green
leaves. May de-
velop edible
fruit. Good
large accent
plant. Likes
sun, regular

M. cavendishii

fertilizing, warm temperatures, high humidity. Plant
in equal parts standard potting mix and peat moss.
Give plenty of water.

M. cavendishii (M. nana). To 5-6 feet tall. Leaves 2-3
feet long, bluish green blotched red while young. Edible
yellow fruit to 5 inches long.

M. coccinea. To 4 feet tall. Bright green leaves to 3
feet long. Bloom has scarlet bracts, yellow tips.

M. mannii. To 2 feet tall. Stem tinged black. Erect
bloom stalk has red bracts, yellow flowers.

M. velutina. To 4 feet tall. Leaves to 3 feet long. In-
edible fruit. M. 'Velutina Hybrid' has red markings on
leaf edges. Flowers with red bracts, yellow flowers.

Neanthe bella. See Chamaedorea elegans.

NEOREGELIA. Epi-
phytic bromeliads na-
tive to tropical Amer-
ica. Many varieties,
different in size and
color. Rosette growth.
Center of plant
("vase") turns crim-
son at bloom time. In-
significant flowers.
Likes bright light,
warm temperatures.
Plant in osmunda fi-
ber or fir bark. Keep
potting mix moist;

have "vase" filled with water. See photo on page 66.

N. carolinae 'Tricolor'. Green and white striped
leaves. Blue flowers.

N. spectabilis. Fingernail plant. Pale green leaves
with red tips. Blue flowers in summer.

NEPHROLEPIS. Sword
fern. Easily grown ferns.
Sword-shaped fronds with
closely spaced leaflets.
Likes bright light (no direct sun), average house
temperatures, some hu-
midity, regular fertilizing,
good drainage. Plant in
equal parts standard pot-
ting mix and peat moss.

N. exaltata 'Bostoniense'

Keep potting mix moist (should be checked daily in
warm weather); never let roots dry out completely. Can
divide large plants. See photos on pages 71, 75, and
back cover.

N. exaltata 'Bostoniense'. Boston fern. Graceful
drooping fronds. A hybrid discovered in Cambridge,
Massachusetts, in the 1890s. Long-time favorite.

N. e. 'Fluffy Ruffles'. Upright growing, dark green,
very lacy fronds.

N. e. 'Rooseveltii'. Leaflet margins wavy. Tips have
deep lobes.

N. e. 'Smithii'. More pyramid-shaped, very lacy (almost feathery) fronds.

N. e. 'Verona'. Very fancy. Each leaflet divided and
subdivided.

N. e. 'Whitmanii'. Each leaflet divided, wavy edges.

**NIDULARIUM in-
nocentii.** Brome-
liad native to trop-
ical America.
Straplike, olive
green leaves with
spiny margins; ro-
sette growth. Bril-
liant red, bractlike
leaves form a
smaller, nestlike
rosette in center.
Appropriately, the
name *Nidularium*

means "bird's nest." White flowers rise out of center
in a dense bunch. Likes filtered light, high humidity,
average house temperatures. Plant in osmunda fiber or
fir bark kept moist. Divide when new plant forms near
base.

Strelitzia reginae.
See page 73.

Clerodendrum thomsoniae. *See page 36.*

Plants that bloom indoors

A house plant that flowers indoors is a real treasure, usually indicating a serious and attentive caretaker. To produce blooms inside a house requires strict adherence to your plant's growing needs. The right temperatures, light, humidity, and amounts of water and fertilizer are each important, and, if supplied, will earn you a reward—flowers!

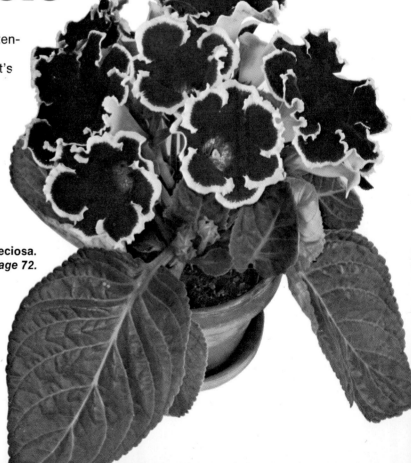

Sinningia speciosa.
See page 72.

Clivia. *See page 36.*

Cymbidium. *See page 40.*

Norfolk Island pine. See Araucaria heterophylla.

NOTOCACTUS. Globe - shaped cactus native to South America. All varieties covered with spines. Flowers in many colors. Likes sun; warm temperatures in summer, cooler (65° or less) during winter. Plant in equal parts standard potting mix and sharp sand. Water when potting mix is dry to touch; give only enough to keep cactus from shrinking in winter.

N. scopa

N. haselbergii. Scarlet ball. Covered with soft, white spines. Red flowers in early spring.

N. mammulosus. Lemon ball. Gray to brown, short-spined, globular, ribbed cactus. Yellow flowers.

N. ottonis. Indian head. Bristly, red brown spines, glossy green globe. Yellow flowers.

N. scopa. Silver ball. Globular, ribbed, covered with soft, white spines. Yellow flowers.

ODONTOGLOSSUM.

This ephiphytic orchid is native to tropical America. Flat, oval pseudobulbs sheathed by small, leathery leaves with two more leaves on top. Ruffled flowers generally in white, yellow, brown, pink. Likes cool temperatures (45°-65° in winter, as low as possible in summer), bright light (no direct sun), high humidity, good ventilation, regular fertilizing. Plant in osmunda fiber or

ground fir bark, let potting mix dry out slightly between waterings. Plants thrive under crowded conditions; keep pot small in relation to plant size.

Old lady cactus. See Mammillaria hahniana.

Old man cactus. See Cephalocereus senilis.

ONCIDIUM. Epiphytic orchids from tropical America. Plant form varies; usually pseudobulbs with leathery leaves (some have pencil-like foliage). Flowers either small and numerous or large and solitary. Likes average to cool temperatures, high humidity, good air circulation, at least 4 hours of sun daily (no direct hot sun). Plant in osmunda fiber or ground fir bark; keep potting mix con-

stantly moist except for several weeks following completion of new growth.

OPUNTIA. Slow-growing cactus. Many kinds with varied appearance, often bizarre. Most species fall into 1 of 2 rather loose categories: the prickly pears with flat, broad joints and the chollas with cylindrical joints. Rarely blooms indoors. Likes warm temperatures in summer (55°-85°), cool temperatures in winter (around 45°); at least 4 hours of sun daily. Plant in equal parts standard potting mix and sharp sand. Let potting mix dry out completely between waterings; in winter, water only to keep plant from shriveling.

O. microdasys

O. basilaris. Beaver tail. Upright, blue green, compact pads. Pink to carmine flowers.

O. microdasys. Bunny ears. Thin, flat, nearly round pads; velvety soft green with neatly spaced tufts of short golden bristles giving a polka dot effect.

O. m. albispina. White bristles. Small new pads atop larger old ones create plant silhouette of an animal's head. A favorite with children.

ORNITHOGALUM caudatum. Pregnant onion, False sea onion. Bulb. Strap - shaped, drooping leaves to 2 feet atop a gray green, smooth-skinned bulb; the greater part of the bulb sits on top of the potting mix. Bulblets form underneath papery outer layer of bulb and swell until they become noticeable bumps, inspiring the nickname "pregnant onion." Eventually the bulblets split the outer layer and fall to the ground, taking root. Tall wands of tiny green and white flowers in April-May. Likes at least 4 hours of sun daily (can

tolerate filtered light), standard potting mix, average house temperatures, regular waterings, occasional fertilizing. Failure to water will cause leaf drop; plants recover when watering is resumed. Do not fertilize or water when bulbs go dormant.

OXALIS. Clover-like leaves. Many species grow from bulbs, tubers. Leaves fold closed at night. Small flowers in pink, white, yellow, rose. Likes a sunny window, standard potting mix, some humidity. Water heavily during growing season. To propagate, divide large plants.

PANDANUS. Screw pine. Native to the South Pacific. Spirally arranged foliage with prickly-edged, spearlike, dark green leaves. Many varieties, some banded with white or silver. Likes standard potting mix, bright light (protect from hot direct sun), warm temperatures, some humidity (likes misting in summer). Water well in summer (drench plant, then let potting mix dry

out); rest plant during winter. With age, develops thick, stiltlike, aerial roots around base. Divide if new shoots form at base.

PAPHIOPEDILUM. Lady's slipper. Terrestrial orchid native to tropical regions of Asia. Usually sold as *Cypripedium.* Graceful, arching foliage (no pseudobulbs) either plain green or mottled. Plain-leafed forms usually flower in winter, mottled-leafed forms in summer. Under this name fall the large-flowered hybrids sold commercially for cut flowers. Many flowers shine as if lacquered. Flowers may be white, yellow, green with white stripes, pure green, or a combination of back-

ground colors with markings in tan, mahogany brown, maroon, green, white. Mottled-leaf forms need 60°-65° nighttime temperatures, 70°-85° during day. Plain-leafed forms require 55°-65° night temperatures, 60°-75° day temperatures. No rest period, so keep plants moist at all times. Plant in equal parts ground bark and sandy loam. Use smallish pots; *Paphiopedilum* thrives when crowded. Repot yearly after bloom. Likes bright light (no direct sun), some humidity, good air circulation. Use weak fertilizers. See photo on page 67.

Papyrus, dwarf. See Cyperus haspan.

Peacock plant. See Calathea makoyana.

PEDILANTHUS tithymaloides. Devil's backbone, Redbird cactus. Succulent. Nicknames come from strange zigzag stems and small, red, birdlike flowers in spring. Lance-shaped leaves are light green with splashes of red, white, and dark green. 'Nanus' a dwarf variety. Likes light from full sun to semishade, average temperatures and humidity, standard potting mix kept evenly moist. To propagate, take stem cutting and allow

it to dry out before placing in rooting mix.

PELARGONIUM. Geranium. Many different flower and leaf forms, some with scented leaves. Flowers in wide range of colors. Keep somewhat potbound for best bloom. When repotting, move to next largest pot size. Likes standard potting mix, a sunny window, warm, dry atmosphere. Water when soil almost dry. Fertilize during active growing season. Pinch out growing tips for bushiness. Don't mist. Propagate by stem cuttings.

PELLAEA. Cliff brake. Small ferns with detailed foliage. Likes standard potting mix with good drainage, filtered light, some humidity. Give lots of water, don't let pot sit in it. See photo, page 70.

   P. rotundifolia. Button fern, Roundleaf fern. Nearly round, dark green leaflets evenly spaced. Good contrast with lacier ferns.

P. viridis

   P. viridis. *(P. adiantoides).* Long fronds to 2 feet. Fresh green, oval to lance-shaped leaflets on brownish black stems.

PEPEROMIA. Evergreen, often succulent, plants with a variety of interesting foliage. Good companion plant in dish gardens. Likes filtered light or a north (sunless) exposure (protect plant from direct sun), standard potting mix with good drainage, high humidity, warm temperatures (will tolerate less), not too much water. Can propagate from stem cuttings. See photo on page 43.

P. caperata 'Emerald Ripple'

   P. 'Astrid'. Apple green, pointed, succulent leaves; compact growth. Long white flower spikes.

   P. caperata 'Emerald Ripple'. Heart-shaped, deeply veined, rich green leaves; short reddish stalks. 'Little Fantasy' a miniature variety.

   P. metallica. Erect, dark red stems; narrow, waxy leaves of copper with a metallic luster and silver green band down leaf center.

   P. obtusifolia. Round, dark green, succulent leaves. 'Minima' is miniature form. 'Variegata' leaves with creamy white margins, light and dark green markings.

   P. polybotrya. Shieldlike, dark green, succulent leaves with white flower stalks.

   P. rotundifolia. Slender, trailing stems; tiny, green, round leaves. Good as ground cover in dish gardens.

   P. sandersii. Watermelon peperomia. Round leaves with gray silver, curved stripes on long stems.

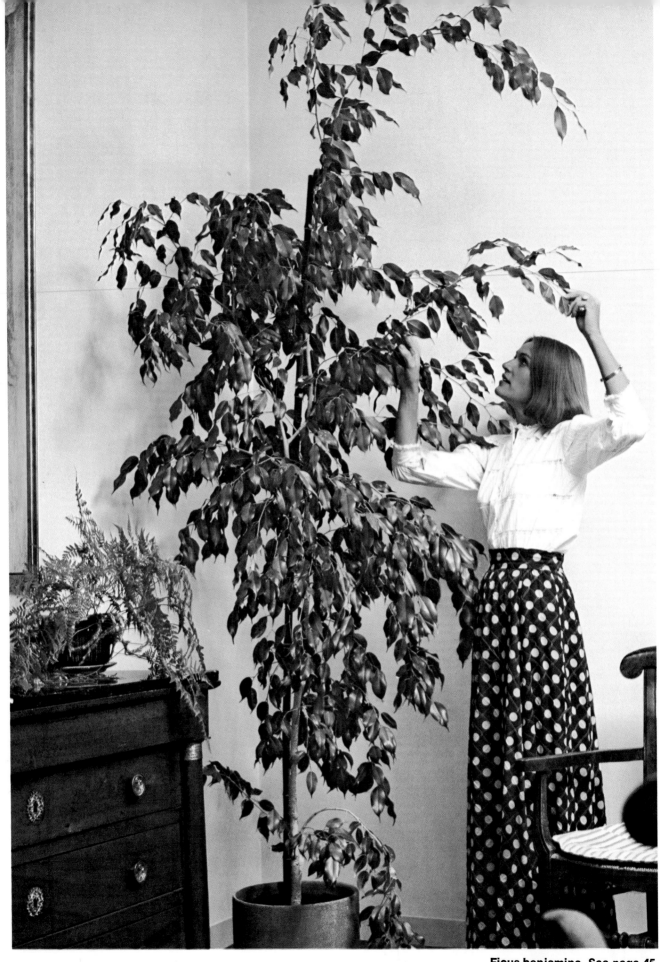

Ficus benjamina. *See page 45.*

Archontophoenix cunninghamiana. *See page 29.*

Put a tree in your house

An indoor tree can serve many purposes: it can fill in empty spaces, hide a multitude of architectural sins, soften harsh interiors. Indoor trees also add a feeling of space and nature. Treat your tree as a permanent fixture, for its size and weight limit flexibility.

Ficus elastica. *See page 45.*

Pseudopanax lessonii. *See page 65.*

PHALAENOPSIS. Moth orchid. Epiphytic orchids native to tropical Asia. Thick, broad, leathery leaves; no pseudobulbs. White and pink-flowered species most widely grown; yellow and multicolored varieties also available. Likes shade (no direct sun), average to warm house temperatures (60° is minimum), high humidity (at least 60 percent). Plant in osmunda fiber or ground fir bark. *Phalaenopsis* should never dry out completely. See photo on page 66.

PHILODEN-DRON. Evergreen vines and shrubs. Tough, durable plants grown for their attractive, leathery, usually glossy leaves. Two main classes: arborescent (relatively hardy) and vining (self-heading and tender). Arborescent *Philodendrons* become big plants with large leaves and sturdy, self-

P. selloum

supporting trunks. Will require more space than most house plants. May be summered outdoors. Vining or self-heading *Philodendrons* are only house plants. Vining types need support. Support can be almost anything, but certain water-absorbent columns (sections of tree fern stems, wire and sphagnum moss "totem poles," slabs of redwood bark) serve well because they can be kept moist. Self-heading types form short, broad plant with sets of leaves radiating out from central point. All *Philodendrons* like standard potting mix with good drainage, average house temperatures, good light but no direct sun, some humidity. All like ample water but will not tolerate soggy soil. Fertilize frequently with light fertilizer mixtures. Aerial roots form on some kinds; push them into the soil or cut them off. Callalike flowers may appear on old plants grown in perfect environment. Flower bracts are usually green, white, or reddish. Most drop lower leaves, exposing stems. Leafy top of plant can be air layered and repotted or plant can be cut back to stub. See photos on page 39.

P. 'Hastatum'. Vining. Fairly fast, open growth. Leaves 1 foot long, arrow-shaped, rich green. Subject to leaf spot if kept too warm, moist.

P. 'Majesty'. Vining. Dark green, almost black, leaves.

P. oxycardium *(P. cordatum)*. Vining. Most common. Deep green, heart-shaped leaves usually 5 inches or less in length on young plants.

P. panduraeforme. Fiddle-leaf philodendron. Vining. Fairly fast climber with rich green, 10-inch leaves oddly lobed to resemble a violin. Sparse foliage on older plants; best planted in multiples.

P. selloum. Arborescent. Leaves to 3 feet, deeply cut. Variety 'Lundii' is more compact.

Piggy-back plant. See Tolmiea menziesii.

PILEA. Juicy-stemmed plants with inconspicuous flowers. Become leggy with too much shade. Likes standard potting mix with good drainage, bright light, average to warm house temperatures, regular fertilizing (once a month) during growing season. Water thoroughly but don't water again until soil surface is dry. Use stem cuttings to propagate. See photo on page 47.

P. involucrata

P. cadierei. Aluminum plant. Erect growth with showy, silver-flecked leaves. 'Minima' is dwarf variety.

P. depressa. Baby's tears. Bright, apple green, tiny, roundish leaves; creeping growth. Good as ground cover in dish gardens, terrariums.

P. involucrata. Panamiga, Panamigo. Glossy, roundish oval, bronze green leaves with purplish undersides, heavily veiled in seersucker effect.

P. microphylla. Artillery plant. Tiny, thick, bright green leaves in fernlike sprays. Prune to keep compact. Nickname comes from habit of "forcibly discharging pollen" (quote from *Standard The Cylopedia of Horticulture* by L. H. Bailey).

P. nummulariaefolia. Creeping Charlie. Creeping habit; small, round, slightly hairy leaves.

P. 'Silver Tree'. Dark olive green leaves with silvery strip down middle.

Pineapple. See Ananas.

Pink polka dot plant. See Hypoestes sanguinolenta.

Pisonia. See Heimerliodendron.

PLATYCERIUM. Staghorn fern. Odd epiphytic fern from tropical regions. Two kinds of fronds: sterile ones (flat, pale green aging to tan and brown, they support plant and accumulate organic matter to help feed it) and fertile fronds (forked, resembling deer antlers for which plant is nicknamed). Can be summered outdoors on shaded patios. In nature it grows on trees; grow it on slabs of bark or tree fern stem; occasionally used in hanging baskets.

Likes bright light, high humidity (mist frequently), average to cool temperatures. Grow in organic matter kept moist at all times. Give it lots of space. May form new plants at shield base. See photo on page 70.

PLECTRANTHUS. Swedish ivy. Trailing perennial from Africa with round, thick, almost succulent leaves. Tiny white flowers on upright spikes. Likes standard potting mix; average temperatures, moisture, and humidity. Tolerates dim light. Fast growing. Good in hanging baskets. Start plants from stem cuttings. See photo on page 46.

P. australis

P. australis. Shiny, dark green leaves.

P. coleoides 'Marginatus'. Dark green leaves with white, toothed, scalloped edges.

P. oertendahlii. Apple green leaves with silver veins, purple underneath. Pinkish flowers.

Poinsettia. See Euphorbia pulcherrima.

POLYPODIUM aureum. Hare's foot fern. Fern native to tropical America. Good in hanging baskets. Leathery fronds with toothed leaves. Heavy, brown, hairy, creeping rhizomes that resemble animals' feet, giving them their nickname. Likes filtered light, potting mix high in organic matter, average temperatures, humidity (mist often — prefers to be kept moist). See photo on page 70.

P. a. undulatum. Large fronds with wavy edges.

POLYSCIAS. Plants related to the *Aralia* family but native to tropical Asia and Polynesia (true *Aralias* are native to China). Touchy, slow growing, sensitive to cold. Needs bright light, regular fertilizing, standard potting mix, high humidity (likes misting). Put in warmest spot in house; keep free of drafts. Water well about once a week when soil is dry to touch.

P. fruticosa 'Elegans'

P. balfouriana. Round, slightly scalloped, solid green leaves.

P.b. 'Marginata'. Round scalloped leaves with white margin. Tolerates either sun or shade.

P. fruticosa 'Elegans'. Ming aralia, Parsley panax. Parsleylike foliage on woody stem.

P. guilfoylei 'Victoriae'. Thin, leathery, curled leaves with white, toothed edges.

P. paniculata 'Variegata'. Roundish, light green leaves with dark green, toothed edges.

POLYSTICHUM. Fern with dark green fronds that form symmetrical plants. Likes standard potting mix with added humus, shade, ample water, average indoor temperatures and humidity.

P. tsus-simense. Dwarf variety to 8 inches with leathery, dark green fronds.

Pothos. See Rhaphidophora aurea.

Powder puff cactus. See Mammillaria bocasana.

Prayer plant. See Maranta leuconeura.

Pregnant onion. See Ornithogalum.

PSEUDOPANAX LESSONII. Evergreen, multistemmed tree native to New Zealand. Leaves dark green, leathery, divided into 3-5 leaflets 1-3 inches long. Can tolerate sun or shade, average house conditions. Let potting mix dry out between waterings. Confined roots keep plant bushy. See photo on page 63.

PTERIS. Brake, Table fern, Ribbon fern, Victoria fern. Tropical ferns best known for forked and crested, green or variegated fronds. Many varieties. Likes filtered light (can tolerate shade), cool temperatures, humidity, ample water.

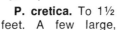
P. cretica

P. cretica. To 1½ feet. A few large, narrow leaflets. Many forms, some variegated, some with forked or crested fronds.

P. ensiformis 'Victoriae'. Silvery white fronds edged in dark green.

P. quadriaurita 'Argyraea'. Silver fern. Native to India. Tall fronds rather coarsely divided, heavily marked with white.

Purple waffle plant. See Hemigraphis.

Queen's tears. See Billbergia nutans.

Rabbit's foot fern. See Davallia fejeenis.

Rabbit tracks. See Maranta leuconeura.

Rattan palm. See Rhapis humilis.

Rattlesnake plant. See Calathea insignis.

(Continued on page 68)

Cymbidium. *See page 40.*

Phalaenopsis. *See page 64.*

Neoregelia carolinae 'Tricolor'. *See page 57.*

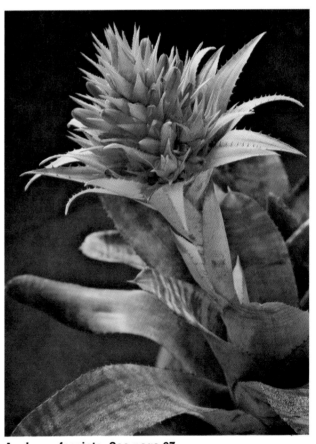

Vriesia splendens 'Major'.
See page 77.

Orchids and bromeliads

Their graceful curves and unusual flower forms—as well as their finicky reputations—put orchids and bromeliads in a category by themselves. Surprisingly, these exotics aren't difficult to grow—just provide their preferences for light, humidity, and water, and then wait for the plaudits.

Paphiopedilum. *See page 61.*

Aechmea fasciata. *See page 27.*

RECHSTEINERIA. Tuberous plants related to African violets. Compact, broad-leafed growth. Narrow, tubular, mostly red flowers. Likes warm temperatures (65° at night, 70° during the day), high humidity, bright light (no direct hot summer sun), regular fertilizing during growing season. Plant in packaged African violet potting mix. Generously water when soil surface dries out; never let roots

dry out. During winter rest period, gradually withhold water until leaves turn yellow; then stop watering until they dry out. Water only enough to keep tubers plump. When new growth starts (or after 3 months dormancy), resume watering and fertilizing.

R. cardinalis. Most common. Broad, heart-shaped, fuzzy leaves grow compactly in opposite pairs. Red flowers in summer. Can have flowers at Christmas if tubers are started in fall.

R. leucotricha. Brazilian edelweiss. Silvery leaves covered with white hairs. Salmon red flowers.

Rex begonia. See Begonia rex-cultorum.

RHAPHIDOPHORA aurea (*Scindapsus aureus, Pothos aureus*). Devil's ivy, Silver pothos. Evergreen, perennial climbers related to *Philodendron,* similar in appearance. Oval, leathery leaves with pale white or yellow splotches. Train to

climb or trail. Good in hanging baskets. Likes standard potting mix, good light, regular watering, fertilizer; will tolerate adverse conditions. To propagate, use stem cuttings. See photo on page 50.

RHAPIS. Lady Palm. Fan palm that forms bamboolike clumps with deep green foliage. Trunks covered with a net of dark, fibrous leaf sheaths. Slow growing; excellent container palm. Likes semishade (can tolerate some sun or poor light), average house temperatures and humidity, regular fertilizing (weak feedings monthly), standard potting mix. Water frequently.

R. excelsa. Slow grower to about 12 feet. Can tolerate poor light, dust, drought.

R. humilis. Rattan palm, Slender lady palm. Tall to about 18 feet. Gives graceful tropical air. Larger, longer leaves than *R. excelsa,* less tolerant of sun.

R. excelsa

RHOEO spathacea. (*R. discolor*). Moses - in - the - cradle, Moses-in-the-boat. Perennial. Sword-shaped, rather erect leaves are dark green with deep purple underneath. Interesting flowers; small, white, 3-petaled, they are crowded into boat-shaped bracts down among the leaves, giving plant its nickname. Tolerant plant

adapts well to adverse conditions. Likes standard potting mix, average house temperatures and humidity, light from high to low ranges, regular to casual watering. 'Vittata' leaves striped red and yellowish green.

Rosary vine. See Ceropegia woodii.

Rubber plant. See Ficus elastica.

RUELLIA makoyana. Trailing velvet plant. A native of Brazil. A low and spreading plant with small, velvety, olive green leaves having purple shadings, silvery veins. Likes high humidity, constant moisture, filtered light, and daytime temperatures above 65°. Use standard potting mix with extra humus. Use stem cuttings for new plants.

SAINTPAULIA ionantha. African violet. Evergreen perennial native to Africa. Probably the most popular house plant in the United States. Fuzzy, heart-shaped, dark green leaves with smooth edges grow in rosettes. Pale lavender flowers in clusters of 3

or more. Hybrids and named varieties have leaves that are plain or scalloped, green or variegated; flowers that are purple, violet, pink, white, cerise, or variegated. Likes very bright light (can take some sun during fall, winter, spring; will grow under artificial light), high humidity, average house temperatures (never below 60°), good air circulation. Plant in packaged African violet potting mix. Water thoroughly from top to bottom with room temperature water; let soil surface become dry between waterings. Don't let water sit in saucer for more than 2 hours. Use smallish pots; African violets bloom best with crowded roots. Fertilize regularly once every 2-4 weeks (there are commercial fertilizers formulated especially for African violets; follow label directions carefully); be sure soil is moist before fertilizing. For more information, see *Sunset* book *How to Grow African Violets.* Use leaf cuttings to propagate. See photo on page 59.

SANSEVIERIA. Bowstring hemp, Snake plant, Mother-in-law's tongue. Evergreen perennial succulent native to Africa, India. Thick, patterned leaves grow in clusters and radiate up and out from base, range in shape from short, blunt triangles to long swords. First nickname comes from use of tough fibers in leaves as bowstrings; second comes from banding or mottling on leaves that causes them to resemble snakeskin; third probably comes from toughness of leaves and plants' persistence under neglect. Clusters of greenish white flowers seldom appear. Likes standard potting mix, average house conditions. Light may vary from bright to low. Water thoroughly but infrequently. Tolerates dry air, uneven temperatures, capricious watering. Propagate from portion of a leaf.

S. trifasciata

S. 'Hahnii'. Broad, fleshy, 6-inch, dark green leaves cross-banded with irregular silvery markings. Good in small pots, dish gardens.

S. trifasciata *(S. zeylanica).* Leaves 1-4 feet long, 2 inches or more wide; fleshy, dark green, banded with silvery gray. Variety 'Laurentii' is best known.

SAXIFRAGA stolonifera *(S. sarmentosa).* Strawberry geranium, Strawberry begonia. Creeping perennial native to China, Japan. Forms runners like those of strawberry plants, producing new plantlets at stem ends. Fuzzy, white-veined, nearly round, green leaves with pink underneath. White flowers in clusters on tall stems. Good in hanging baskets. Likes filtered light, standard potting mix, cool temperatures, some humidity, considerable moisture.

S. s. 'Tricolor'. Green leaves liberally edged in white with pink underneath.

Schefflera. See Brassaia actinophylla.

SCHEFFLERA arboricola. Fast-growing, evergreen, tropical-looking plant with long-stalked leaves divided into leaflets which spread like the fingers of a hand. Likes good soil, ample water, average house conditions. Will tolerate either sun or shade. See photo on page 43.

SCHLUMBER-GERA. Epiphytic cactus (cactus that lives in trees like certain orchids) native to tropics. Plants often confused in nursery trade; many hybrids, selections differ in color. Plant in rich, porous soil with plenty of leaf mold, sand.

Likes bright light, humidity, average house temperatures, frequent watering and fertilizing (feed as often as every 7-10 days). To ensure bloom, give plants a rest in fall; keep cool, dry; give 12 hours of darkness. See photo on back cover.

S. bridgesii *(Zygocactus truncatus).* Christmas cactus. In nature, plant may be 3 feet across, with arching drooping branches made up of flattened, scalloped, smooth, bright green, spineless joints. Many-petaled, tubular, rosy purplish red flowers around Christmas.

S. gaertneri. See *Rhipsalidopsis gaertneri.*

S. truncata *(Zygocactus truncatus).* Crab cactus. Joints 1-2 inches long, sharply toothed, with 2 large teeth at end of last joint. Short-tubed flowers with spreading, pointed, scarlet petals. Blooms November-March. Many varieties in white, pink, salmon, orange.

Scindapsus. See Rhaphidophora aurea.

Screw pine. See Pandanus.

SEDUM. Stonecrop. Succulents that come from many parts of the world and vary in hardiness and growing needs. Some tiny and trailing, others upright. Fleshy leaves highly variable in size, shape, color; evergreen varieties best indoors. Plant in equal parts standard potting mix and sharp sand. Likes bright light. See photo on page 79.

S. morganianum

S. adolphii. Short, fleshy, yellow green leaves tinged red.

S. brevifolium. Native to Europe, North Africa. Tiny, slow-growing, tightly packed, fleshy leaves, gray white flushed red. Flowers pinkish or white. Sunburns in hot dry spots. Needs good drainage.

S. dasyphyllum. Blue gray leaves; hairy white flowers.

S. morganianum. Donkey tail, Burro tail. Can be summered outdoors. Long trailing stems to 3-4 feet. Thick, fleshy, light gray green leaves overlapping on stem, giving a braided or ropelike effect. Good in hanging baskets. Likes filtered light. Water freely (needs good drainage); fertilize 2 or 3 times during summer. 'Burrita' is small, compact version.

S. multiceps. Miniature "tree" form with needlelike, dark green leaves; yellow flowers.

S. stahlii. Coral beads. Native to Mexico. Trailing growth. Reddish brown leaves set closely together on stem. Yellow flowers in summer or fall.

Seersucker plant. See Geogenanthus.

(Continued on page 72)

Platycerium bifurcatum.
See page 64.

Ferns – plain and fancy

Growing ferns can be habit forming—
for a successful grower, one plant is
rarely enough. Ferns come in a wide
range of shapes and forms, from elegant
Bostons to bizarre staghorns.

Ferns do demand special surround-
ings. Most prefer coolish temperatures,
indirect light, some humidity, and lots of
space—they hate to be crowded.

Polypodium aureum undulatum.
See page 65.

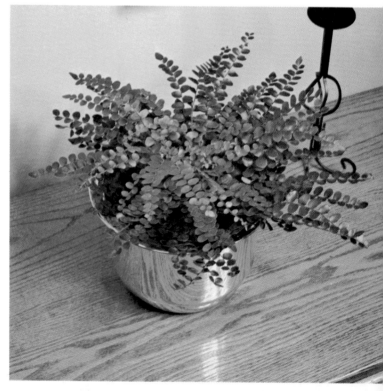

Pellaea rotundifolia.
See page 61.

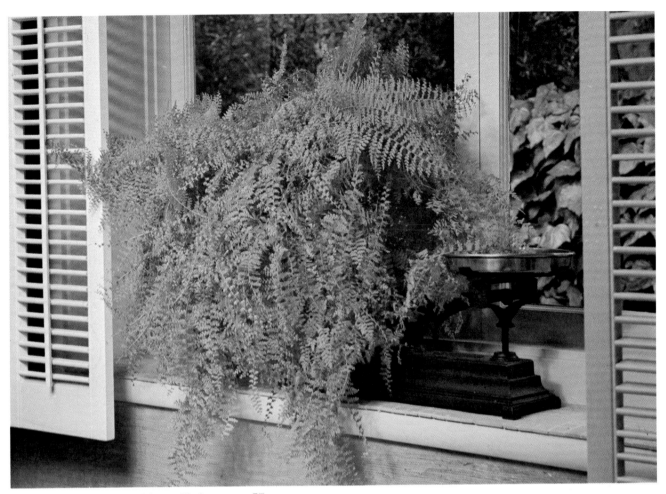

Nephrolepis exaltata 'Whitmanii'. *See page 57.*

Davallia trichomanoides. *See page 41.*

Asplenium nidus. *See page 29.*

SELAGINELLA. Moss fern, Spike moss. Branching, mosslike plant is taller and fluffier than real moss. Creeping growth. Good as ground cover in terrariums, dish gardens. Can trail in hanging baskets. Likes shade, standard potting mix, high humidity, lots of water.

S. kraussiana

S. kraussiana. Dwarf with bright green leaves.
S. k. 'Aurea'. Yellow green.
S. k. brownii. Club moss. Slow spreading. Smallest form about 1 inch. Pale green.
S. uncinata. Peacock fern. Leaves of iridescent metallic blue green.

SEMPERVIVUM. Houseleek. Evergreen perennial succulent with tightly packed rosettes of leaves. Little offsets cluster around parent rosette. Star-shaped flowers in clusters in white, yellowish, pink, red, greenish; summer blooming. Blooming rosettes die after setting seed, but offsets continue. Plant in equal parts standard potting mix and sharp sand. Likes sun, good drainage, lots of water in summer.

S. tectorum

S. montanum. Tightly packed, tiny leaf rosettes.
S. tectorum. Hen and chickens. Gray green rosettes that quickly spread. Leaves tipped red brown, bristle-pointed. Red flowers.

SENECIO. Perennials related to daisy; some succulent. Mostly hardy, adaptable to house conditions. Likes standard potting mix, sun or bright light, average watering, house temperatures, humidity.
S. mikanioides. German ivy. Vining growth; good

S. mikanioides

in hanging baskets. Should be evergreen indoors (can be deciduous in all but mildest climates). Roundish, ivylike leaves with 5-7 sharply pointed lobes. Small yellow flowers in winter. Prune to control size.
S. rowleyanus. String of beads. Succulent. Trailing or hanging stems set with ½-inch, spherical, green leaves that resemble beads. Good in hanging baskets. Small, white, carnation-scented flowers.

Sensitive plant. See Mimosa pudica.

Sentry palm. See Howeia belmoreana.

Shrimp plant. See Beloperone guttata.

Sickle-thorn asparagus. See Asparagus falcatus.

SIDERASIS fuscata. Rosette of oval green leaves with velvety red hairs and a white midrib; purple underneath. Likes standard potting mix with extra humus added, cool to average temperatures (60° - 70°), bright light. Water when soil surface dries out.

Silver dollar. See Crassula arborescens.

Silver fern. See Pteris quadriaurita 'Argyraea'.

SINNINGIA speciosa. (Gloxinia speciosa). Gloxinia. Tuberous plant native to South American tropics. Related to African violet. Tubers usually available December-March. Large, oblong, dark green, toothed, fuzzy leaves to 6 inches or more. Large flowers, velvety, bell-shaped, ruffled on edges, in purple,

blue, violet, pink, red, white. Some flowers have dark spots or blotches. Plant tubers in packaged African violet potting mix with sand added: 3 parts mix to 1 part sand. Tuberous plants normally go dormant; when plant stops growing (no new leaves or flowers), withhold water until leaves turn yellow; then stop watering so they will dry out. Dormancy lasts for 1½-3 months; give only enough water to prevent tuber from shriveling and soil from completely drying out. Store at about 60°. When new growth begins, repot or plant tuber 1 inch below soil surface (be sure indented top side faces up). Water moderately until roots are established; then water generously. Allow soil surface to dry out between waterings. Likes high humidity, temperatures from 65°-75°, bright light, regular fertilizing every 2-4 weeks during growing season. See photo on page 58.

SMITHIANTHA (*Naegelia*). Temple bells. Native to mountain regions in Mexico, Guatemala. Grows from rhizomes. Heart-shaped leaves with densely hairy, velvety leaves. Bell-shaped flowers that hang down like bells in wide range of colors and color combinations. Likes coolish temperatures (60°-70°), filtered light, high humidity, lots of water (never let soil dry out completely). When plants go dormant (usually in fall), withhold water and let

S. zebrina

rhizomes dry out; store in cool place for about 3 months. When new growth starts, repot and return to bright light, regular watering. Plant in packaged African violet potting mix.

S. cinnabarina. Green leaves with velvety red hairs; leaves appear red. Brick red flowers.

S. multiflora. Velvety green leaves, lighter green underneath. Cream-colored or white flowers.

S. zebrina. Leaves with veins marked brown or purple. Red flowers with red-spotted, yellow throats.

Snake plant. See Sansevieria.

Snowflake tree. See Trevesia.

SOLANUM pseudo-capsicum. Jerusalem cherry. Evergreen shrub native to tropics. Deep green, smooth, shiny leaves to 4 inches. White flowers followed by red fruit (rarely yellow) like miniature tomatoes, October-December. Colorful at Christmas time. Fruits may be poisonous. Usually grown as an annual. Pinch and prune frequently to control growth. Many dwarf varieties. Likes

bright light (some sun), average temperatures, standard potting mix, regular watering and fertilizing.

SOLEIROLIA soleirolii *(Helxine soleirolii).* Baby's tears, Angel's tears. Native to Corsica, Sardinia. Creeping, mosslike plants with tiny, round, medium green leaves that form a thick mat. Inconspicuous flowers. Fast growing; pruning encourages more growth. Likes shade or filtered light,

standard potting mix, cool temperatures, high humidity, ample water (won't tolerate standing in water). Use in small containers or as ground cover in terrariums, dish gardens. Divide clumps to propagate.

SPATHIPHYLLUM. White flag. Evergreen perennial. Leaf stalks rise directly from soil. Dark green, large, oval leaves narrow to a point. White flowers resemble calla lilies. Blooms readily indoors. Likes bright light (no direct hot sun), high humidity, frequent watering, regular fertilizing, loose, fibrous potting mix. Commonly available: *S. wallisii, S. 'Mauna Loa', S. 'Clevelandii'*—all similar in appearance. Divide into

clumps to propagate. See photo on page 39.

Spider plant. See Chlorophytum comosum.

Split-leaf philodendron. See Monstera.

Squirrel's foot fern. See Davallia trichomanoides.

Staghorn fern. See Platycerium.

STAPELIA. Starfish flower, Carrion flower. Succulent resembling cactus with clumps of 4-sided, spineless stems. Can be summered outdoors. Flowers in summer are large, fleshy, star-shaped with 5 points; usually have an elaborate circular disk in cen-

S. variegata

ter. Most flowers smell like carrion; not too offensive outdoors. Needs a cool, dry rest period in winter. Likes filtered light, standard potting mix, average house conditions. Moderate watering during growing season.

S. gigantia. Novelty with 9-inch stems. Flowers 10-16 inches across, brown purple marked yellow with fringed edges.

S. variegata. Most common. Stems to 6 inches. Flowers 3 inches across, yellow heavily spotted and barred with dark purple brown. Many hybrids and color variants. Unscented flowers.

STEPHANOTIS floribunda. Madagascar jasmine. Evergreen vine native to Malagasy. Can be summered outdoors. Leaves glossy, dark green, waxy, to 4 inches. Funnel-shaped flowers white, waxy, very fragrant, in open clusters. Outdoors, blooms June through summer; grown indoors and given proper rest by some drying out, will bloom 6 weeks after resuming growth. Outdoors, keep roots in shade, tops in filtered sun. Indoors, likes bright light (no direct sun), some support (frame or trellis), liberal water and fertilizer. If

summered outdoors, let dry out somewhat before bringing indoors. Scale, mealybug common pests.

Stoneface. See Lithops.

Strawberry begonia. See Saxifraga.

STRELITZIA reginae. Bird of paradise . Can be summered outdoors. Tropical evergreen perennial. Leathery, long-stalked, blue green leaves to 1½ feet in clumps. Large, crowded clumps bloom best. Orange, blue, and white flowers on long, stiff stems bloom intermittently throughout the year; resemblance to tropical birds gives nickname. Likes sun (light shade in hot areas), average to warm temperatures, frequent heavy fertilizing, regular watering. See photo on page 58.

(Continued on page 76)

Fill in with big plants

If your house has large expanses of blank walls or empty spaces, consider filling the void with plants. Large house plants can be an inexpensive and attractive solution to this decorating problem, and they are low-maintenance items. Good-size plants need regular watering but less fertilizer and lower light levels than many house plants, since their major growth has already been completed. You can treat them like pieces of art or furniture; just remember to dust them occasionally.

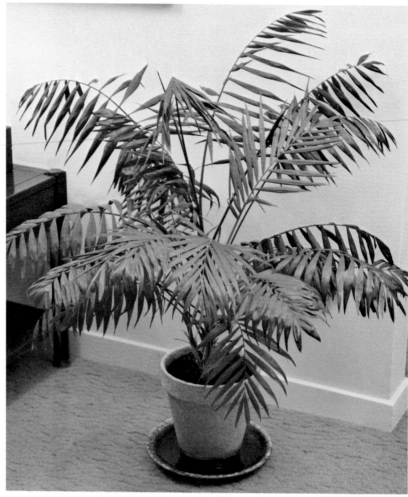

Chamaedorea elegans.
See page 33.

Asparagus retrofractus.
See page 29.

Ctenanthe compressa. *See page 40.*

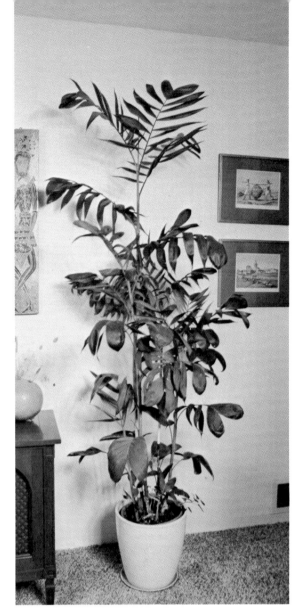

Chamaedorea costaricana. *See page 33.*

Begonia rex-cultorum. *See page 30.*

Nephrolepis exaltata 'Bostoniense'. *See page 57.*

STREPTOCARPUS.
Cape primrose. Evergreen perennials native to South Africa. Related to African violets. Many species that vary in size, shapes of leaves, flowers. Leaves large, fleshy, sometimes velvety. Flowers trumpet-shaped with long tube and spreading mouth, fall-winter bloom. Buy plants or grow from seed. Likes cool temperatures (55°-60°),

bright light (no direct sun), packaged African violet potting mix. Keep moist. Hybrids most common in nurseries, seed catalogs: giant hybrids with flowers in white, blue, pink, rose, red, often with contrasting blotches; Wiesmoor hybrids with flowers fringed, crested, many colors. See photo on page 54.

S. saxorum. Very hairy 1-inch leaves on trailing stems. White-throated, lavender flowers.

String of beads. See Senecio rowleyanus.

String of hearts. See Ceropegia woodii.

SUCCULENT. A succulent is any plant that stores water in juicy leaves, stems, or roots to withstand drought. Epiphytic orchids and cactus are commonly excluded from this group. Most succulents are native to desert or semidesert areas in warmer parts of the world; Mexico and South Africa are two important sources. Some (such as sedums and sempervivums) come from colder climates, where they grow on dry rocky ledges. Most are easy to grow and require little care. Not all like hot sun; read species descriptions carefully. For succulents to grow indoors, see *Agave, Aloe, Ceropegia woodii, Crassula, Echeveria, Euphorbia, Gasteria, Haworthia, Kalanchoe, Lithops, Sansevieria, Sedum, Sempervivum.*

Swedish ivy. See Plectranthus.

Sword fern. See Nephrolepis.

SYNGONIUM podophyllum *(Nephthytis).* Arrowhead plant. Evergreen, slow-growing shrub related to *Philodendron.* Can be trained to climb, hang, grow upright with support. Has aerial

roots. Easy to grow. Arrow-shaped, long-stalked, dull green or variegated leaves. Likes standard potting mix, lots of water (can be rooted in water; will live there for unlimited period), average house temperatures and humidity, regular fertilizing. Can take most light situations: with lots of light, leaves are bright green, large; in darker spots, leaves are darker, smaller, variegated leaves are more patterned. Prune to make bushy. Good

in dish gardens, terrariums. Many varieties: 'Ruth Fraser', silvery leaves bordered green; 'Trileaf Wonder', green leaves covered with whitish powder; 'California Silver Wonder', narrow, silvery leaves. Propagate by stem cuttings. See photo on page 54.

Tahitian bridal veil. See Tradescantia multiflora.

Taro. See Colocasia esculenta.

Ti. See Cordyline terminalis.

Tiger orchid. See Odontoglossum.

TILLANDSIA lindeniana *(Vriesia lindenii).* Epiphytic bromeliad with rosette form. Large flower spike has crimson bracts overlapping dense, flattened plume with small, bluish purple flowers. Plant in osmunda fiber, fir bark, or in a tree branch with a pocket of sphagnum moss. Likes bright light (no direct hot sun), average temperatures, good air circulation, regular fertilizing. Let

potting mix dry out between waterings.

TOLMIEA menziesii.
Piggy-back plant, Pick-a-back. Native to coastal mountain ranges from northern California northward to Alaska. Heart-shaped, apple green leaves

with delicate fuzz and toothed edges. New plantlets grow on top of older leaves (at junction of leaf stalk and blade), giving nickname. Inconspicuous reddish brown flowers. Likes filtered light, cool temperatures, standard potting mix, average indoor humidity, lots of water. Variegated variety has yellowish blotches on the leaves. See photos on pages 35 and 47.

TRADESCANTIA. Wandering Jew, Inch plant. Perennial vine from Central and South America. Grown for foliage. Fast growing. Needs frequent pruning to control size, keep compact. Succulent stems with swollen joint where oval or oblong leaves attach. Likes standard potting mix, light ranging from sun to shade, average house conditions, normal watering. Good for

T. multiflora

hanging baskets. Use stem cuttings to propagate. See photo on page 55.

T. fluminensis. Dark green, 2½-inch-long, oval leaves. Tiny white flowers. 'Variegata' has leaves striped yellow or white.

T. multiflora *(Tripogandra multiflora).* Tahitian bridal veil. Purplish green foliage with tiny, white, delicate flowers. Needs filtered light; no direct sun.

Tree fern, Hawaiian. See Cibotium.

TREVESIA. Snowflake tree. Evergreen shrub, small tree. Resembles *Fatsia japonica* in growth habit but taller (10-20) feet, more tree-like. Leaves on long stalks, 1-2 feet across, deeply cut and lobed, resembling outline of enormous snowflake. Likes bright light (no direct hot sun from west or south exposure), standard potting mix with good drainage, liberal watering and fertilizing, average house conditions. Mealybug, spider mite may be a problem.

Tripogandra multiflora. See Tradescantia multiflora.

Turtle orchid. See Oncidium.

Umbrella plant. See Cyperus alternifolius.

Umbrella tree. See Brassaia actinophylla.

VANDA. Epiphytic orchid native to the Philippines, Malaysia, the Himalayas; now grown commercially in the Hawaiian Islands. Plants grow erect with leaves arranged opposite each other. Open-faced flowers. Plant in osmunda fiber or ground fir bark. Stem needs support to anchor aerial roots. Likes warm temperatures (60° is maximum low), high humidity, good air circulation, lots of bright light, especially from November to February to set flower buds. Water lightly during winter.

V. teres

V. caerulea. Native to India. Large, 3-4-inch flowers from pale to dark blue on long stems; blooms late summer, early fall. Dark green, rigid leaves.

V. sanderiana. To 3 feet. Flat, 3-4-inch flowers in fall; combination of white, rose, greenish yellow, brown, dark red.

V. teres. Native to Burma. Flowers used in making leis in Hawaii. Flowers shades of rose with tinges of white, yellow; blooms from May to September. Needs winter rest, tremendous amounts of light.

Velvet plant. See Gynura aurantiaca.

Velvet plant, trailing. See Ruellia makoyana.

Venus flytrap. See Dionaea muscipula.

VRIESIA. Bromeliad with rosette growth. Feathery flower plumes. Some foliage mottled, banded brown. Likes bright light (no direct hot sun), good air circulation, average house temperatures and humidity. Keep "vase" filled with water. Let potting mix dry out slightly between waterings. Divide when new plant forms at base. See photo on page 67.

V. 'Mariae'

V. 'Mariae'. Light green leaves. Yellow flowers rise in clusters, are encased in bracts that are red at base, yellow dotted with brown at tip.

V. splendens 'Major'. Dark green leaves banded with deep reddish purple underneath, lighter on top. Flowers yellowish white encased in red bracts.

Waffle plant. See Hemigraphis.

Wandering Jew. See Tradescantia fluminensis, Zebrina pendula.

Watermelon peperomia. See Peperomia sandersii.

Wax begonia. See Begonia semperflorens.

Wax flower. See Hoya.

Weeping fig. See Ficus benjamina.

White flag. See Spathiphyllum.

Zebra basket vine. See Aeschynanthus marmoratus.

Zebra plant. See Calathea zebrina.

ZEBRINA pendula. Wandering Jew. Evergreen trailing plant native to tropical Mexico and Central America. Same growth habit and leaf shape as *Tradescantia fluminensis* but not as hardy. Many variegated forms. Likes standard potting mix, some humidity, ample water. Variegated leaf forms need more light than all-green ones. Use stem cuttings to propagate.

Z. p. 'Quadricolor'. Purplish green leaves with longitudinal bands of white, pink, carmine red.

ZYGOCACTUS truncatus. Two plants have been sold under this name. For the best known of these—Christmas cactus—see *Schlumbergera bridgesii.* For the Crab cactus, see *Schlumbergera truncata.*

Mammillaria bocasana. *See page 56.*

Cactus and succulents

If you want house plants that can tolerate a warm, dry location and casual care, consider the cactus and succulents. Most of these hardy plants will thrive in average house conditions with minimum amounts of water and fertilizer. Some, though, are more exacting in their requirements and will need more attention—the Plant Section Guide will help you choose. Most cactus and succulents do require good light. They grow slowly and are shallow rooted, so repotting should be done infrequently.

Crassula argentea 'Sunset'.
See page 37.

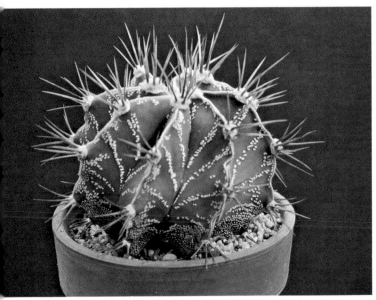

Astrophytum capricorne. *See page 30.*

Sedum morganianum 'Burrita'. *See page 69.*

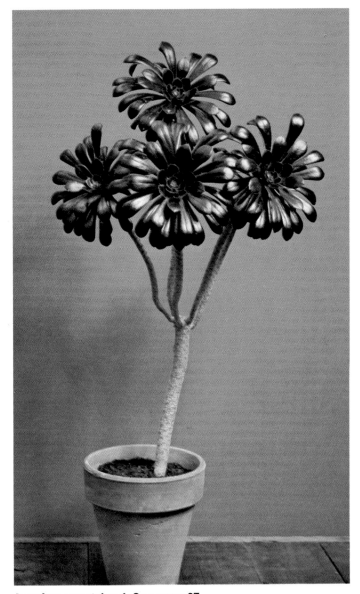

Aeonium swartzkopf. *See page 27.*

Lobivia ferox. *See page 56.*

Index

To find an individual plant description, look up the plant name, listed alphabetically in the Plant Selection Guide, pages 26-79. This index gives page numbers for general house plant information only.

Photographers

The majority of the photographs in this book and those on the back cover are by **Ells Marugg.** Other photographers and their pages: **Glenn Christiansen,** 62; **Gerald R. Frederick,** 34 top left; **Don Normark,** 4, 14; **Norman A. Plate,** 26; **Darrow M. Watt,** 8, 22.

Sunset Books

BUILDING BOOKS

- Basic Carpentry Illustrated 2.45
- Basic Home Repairs Illustrated 2.45
- Basic Plumbing Illustrated 2.45
- Bathrooms 2.45
- Bookshelves & Cabinets 2.45
- Building Barbecues 2.45
- Cabins and Vacation Houses 2.45
- Children's Rooms and Play Yards 2.45
- Decks 2.45
- Fences and Gates 2.45
- Fireplaces 2.45
- Furniture Finishing and Refinishing . . . 2.45
- Furniture Upholstery and Repair 2.45
- Furniture You Can Make 2.45
- Garden & Patio Building 2.45
- Garden Pools, Fntns, Waterfalls 2.45
- Kitchens 2.45
- Leisure Rooms 2.45
- Paneling, Painting & Wallpapering . . . 2.45
- Patio Book 2.45
- Patio Roofs 2.45
- Planning Your New Home 2.45
- Remodeling Your Home 2.45
- Storage 2.45
- Swimming Pools 2.45
- Tables and Chairs: Easy-to-Make 2.45
- Walks, Walls, & Patio Floors 2.45

COOK BOOKS

- Barbecue Cook Book 2.45
- Breads 2.45
- Casserole Book 2.45
- Chafing Dish & Fondue Cook Book . . . 2.45
- Favorite Recipes 2.45
- French Cook Book 2.45
- Ground Beef Recipes 2.45
- Home Canning 2.45
- Hors d'oeuvres 2.45
- Italian Cook Book 2.45
- Low-Cost Cookery 2.45
- Mexican Cook Book 2.45
- Microwave Cook Book 2.45
- Oriental Cook Book 2.45
- Quick & Easy Dinners 2.45

- Salad Book 2.45
- Scandinavian Cook Book 2.45
- Seafood Cook Book 2.45
- Soups & Stews 2.45
- Spices & Herbs 2.45
- Vegetable Cook Book 2.45
- Wine Cook Book 2.45

CRAFT BOOKS

- Ceramics 2.45
- Children's Crafts 2.45
- Crochet 2.45
- Jewelry You Can Make 2.45
- Knitting 2.45
- Leather 2.45
- Macrame 2.45
- Needlepoint 2.45
- Quilting & Patchwork 2.45
- Stitchery 2.45
- Things to Make for Children 2.45
- Weaving 2.45
- Woodcarving 2.45
- Woodworking Projects 2.45

GARDENING BOOKS

- African Violets 2.45
- Annuals 2.45
- Attracting Birds to Your Garden 2.45
- Basic Gardening Illustrated 2.45
- Bonsai 2.45
- Bulbs 2.45
- Color In Your Garden 2.45
- Garden Trees 2.45
- Gardening in Containers 2.45
- Greenhouse Gardening 2.45
- Hanging Gardens 2.45
- Herbs 2.45
- House Plants 2.45
- Landscaping 2.45
- Lawns and Ground Covers 2.45
- Low Maintenance Gardening 2.45
- Orchids 2.45
- Organic Gardening 2.45
- Plant Containers You Can Make 2.45
- Pruning Handbook 2.45

- Rhododendrons and Azaleas 2.45
- Roses 2.45
- Succulents and Cactus 2.45
- Terrariums & Miniature Gardens 2.45
- Vegetable Gardening 2.45
- ★ Desert Gardening 2.45
- ★★ Western Garden Book, Softcover Edition 5.95

*For Arizona, Nevada, New Mexico, Southern California, West Texas
**For Arizona, California, Idaho, Nevada, Oregon, Utah, Washington

TRAVEL BOOKS

- Alaska 2.95
- Arizona 2.95
- Australia 3.95
- Earthquake Country: California 3.95
- Europe 3.95
- Gold Rush Country 2.95
- Hawaii 2.95
- How to Fish the Pacific Coast 3.95
- Islands of the South Pacific 3.95
- Japan 3.95
- Mexico 2.95
- Northern California 2.95
- Oregon 2.95
- Orient 3.95
- Southeast Asia 3.95
- Southern California 2.95
- State Parks: California 2.95
- Washington 2.95
- Wine Country: California 2.95

Available at your local book retailer or use this handy coupon for ordering

Please send me the books I have checked above. I am enclosing $_____ plus 25¢ for postage and handling. Send check or money order—no cash or C.O.D's please.
California residents please add sales tax.

Name_____

Address_____

City_____ State_____ Zip_____

This offer expires 12/77.   60A09